D0477482

KA 0060665 0

BASIC BOOKS IN EDUCATION

Editor: *Kathleen O'Connor, B.Sc., Senior Lecturer in Education, Rolle College, Exmouth*
Advisory Editor: *D. J. O'Connor, M.A., Ph.D., Professor of Philosophy, University of Exeter*

# School Counselling

At a time when counselling is becoming an increasingly important aspect of school life, there is a great need and demand for factual information and practical guidance in this comparatively new field. Mr. Taylor draws on his considerable experience as an educational psychologist to outline and make a case for the specially trained group within the educational professions concerned with counselling. His book examines the role of the school counsellor primarily as a personal adviser. He emphasises the need for a counsellor to be aware of, and involved in, testing programmes and the relevance of psychological theory to counselling practice. He also demonstrates the ways in which a knowledge of sociology enables the counsellor to appreciate the family background of the children in his care.

There are summaries, notes and 'further reading' lists at the end of each chapter, and there is a full bibliography, glossary and index.

# School Counselling

H. J. F. TAYLOR, M.A. (Cantab.)
SENIOR EDUCATIONAL PSYCHOLOGIST
LONDON BOROUGH OF HILLINGDON

MACMILLAN

*First published 1971*

*Published by*
MACMILLAN EDUCATION LTD
*Basingstoke and London*

*Companies and representatives*
*throughout the world*

*Printed in Great Britain by*
ROBERT MACLEHOSE AND CO LTD
*The University Press, Glasgow*

# Foreword

As both society and education become more complex, old roles differentiate and change. This is particularly true of those professions whose principal concern is other human beings. Historically one can see, in professions like medicine, religion, care for children and families in need, two lines of development. The first is a tendency to specialisms within the broad fields; the second is the professionalisation of activities which have hitherto been an unobtrusive part of the social tissue. More recent developments in the climate of our society have profoundly changed the underlying philosophy of the social professions and their differentiated specialisms. The old basis in more or less enlightened and authoritarian paternalism, is now tending to be less acceptable and stress is laid on participation by the client in the process of finding his own way. The doctor, teacher, psychologist, social worker, vocational or personal counsellor is a consultant, an aide or auxiliary rather than an authority or father figure. His aim is that of reconciling aspirations with possibilities, of providing a wide range of information and of communicating this in an assimilable form.

Not entirely paradoxically, this calls for more knowledge and a greater expertise in the social professions—and particularly those developing in novel fields where existing professions have long traditions. School counselling which, as Mr Taylor points out, is a phrase with many nuances of meaning is one such, partaking of a specialisation arising out of the general teaching role and of the professionalisation of activities ordinarily (but now not entirely adequately) discharged casually by many people around the school child and adolescent.

Mr Taylor has undertaken the exceptionally difficult task of outlining—and at the same time making a case for—a specially trained professional group within the educational professions and concerned with counselling. He has indicated the great variety of needs and the corresponding bodies of theory and research in the social and educational sciences, without crystallising upon any of the overlapping concepts beginning to arise in the field. This is all to the good. All those concerned with education will have to give serious thought to guidance and counselling over the next decade and to tease out the functions to be discharged as well as to devise roles and appropriate training and supportive services. One thing is certain. Great flexibility will have to be the rule; and school psychological services, services of remedial education, of child and vocational guidance, school medical services, school welfare, child care and others surrounding the school will have to consider together how their professional and disciplinary boundaries can cease to be jealously guarded frontiers and become (like the new partitionless schools) areas of open access and common work. In this school counselling might well have the critical part to play.

May I then recommend this book written by an experienced educational psychologist with a long and intimate experience of the schools and their needs to all student teachers, teachers in practice, trainers of teachers and particularly to those in professions adjacent to the schools.

W. D. WALL

# Contents


| | | |
|---|---|---|
| | *Acknowledgements* | *page* 8 |
| | *Preface* | 9 |
| 1 | Schools, Guidance and Counselling | 10 |
| 2 | The Counsellor Inside and Outside the School | 34 |
| 3 | Psychological Theory and the Counsellor | 55 |
| 4 | Aspects of Appraisal in School | 74 |
| 5 | Individual and Group Counselling | 98 |
| 6 | Families and the Counselling of Children with Special Needs | 120 |
| | *Glossary* | 142 |
| | *Appendices A-E* | 144 |
| | *Bibliography* | 153 |
| | *Index* | 159 |

# Acknowledgements

My thanks are due to many who gave generously of their time both in reading drafts and in discussion; to Dr W. D. Wall for his suggestions and kind recommendations; to Dr R. P. M. Urquhart for his diligence and critical acumen in commenting on an early draft; to my colleagues, Miss A. M. Dunne and Miss R. Reynolds for their discussions and helpful comments; to Derek Wright, Lecturer in the Psychology Department of Leicester University, for his skill and time in commenting on a final version. I have drawn freely on their suggestions but absolve them completely from responsibility for what now appears here. I wish to thank, too, the librarian, Mr D. J. Foskett, and his staff at the Institute of Education, London University, for their helpfulness and forbearance. I would like to thank Miss E. M. Sheppard for her skill in deciphering my handwriting and both she and Mrs J. M. Grundy for their typing. Finally, I owe a particular debt to Mrs Kathleen O'Connor for detailed and helpful criticism.

H. J. F. T.
April, 1970.

# Preface

This book grew out of a course for senior staff of secondary schools in the London borough of Hillingdon which I organised in 1966 at the 'Battle of Britain House' at Northwood, Middlesex. This course was entitled 'Problems of Communication and of Personal Development' and was opened by the then Director of the National Foundation for Educational Research, Dr W. D. Wall. The lecturers included Mrs Rose Hacker, Dr James Hemming, Mr James Kitses, Mr Derek Wright and many others. From the discussions it seemed obvious to many that a person was needed in every school who had the time, training, qualifications and personality to deal with young people in a 'counselling' situation and to help in the establishment of a guidance system within the school. The school or educational counsellor seemed to be the natural professional to fulfil this task.

Although I have in mind in this book mostly the development of counselling in the secondary school yet the outline of the principles and problems which the school counsellor faces have some relevance to the primary school. I have not sought to draw too rigid a distinction between the two. I assume that the counsellor's main role will be personal counselling (chapters 2 and 5 discuss this in some detail), yet he must also be knowledgeable about, and involved in, testing programmes (chapter 4) and careers guidance (chapter 2). A knowledge of some psychological theories of development is essential for approaching day-to-day problems (chapter 3). Sociological and psychological knowledge is of relevance to understanding the family background of the young people he sees (chapter 6).

No one person can cover the whole field adequately and I am aware of a rather severe selection of topics, none of which have I been able to deal with in any depth. I am writing primarily for those students in colleges of education who wish for a first acquaintance in this relatively new field in British education. I have not given all the book and article references that might be useful to the student, for mostly I have been content with suggesting wherever possible, the most recent works which themselves have good bibliographies and adequate references to the classics or standard works in educational and counselling psychology.

Although the school counsellor appears a foreign intruder—and most research and current practice is American—yet this is not really so. Many teachers, and others, in this country have been highly skilled practitioners of counselling for a long time but it is only very recently that the benefits of systematic selection and training have been realised. On the other hand, there is much to learn from the American experience because many of their problems and difficulties in developing school counselling seem likely to appear in this country.

Counselling looks like yet another new fad or fashion in education. Its justification lies in an awareness that many psychological needs are not met, and that the changing social context is forcing a re-arrangement of our ideas about human development which creates new demands on educators and young people.

Teaching involves many different functions—those of the music and drama specialist, the remedial teacher, the art specialist, the administrator and so on—and now we have the school counsellor. He has yet to find a place in schools in terms of status, salary and an adequate career structure *vis-à-vis* his colleagues and for the moment many of these problems remain unresolved.

I believe that counselling is central to all approaches to guidance and those involved in everyday work with children and young people have to draw on a reservoir of skills involving many different approaches. I have been content with suggesting spheres of influence that seem to be relevant to a counsellor's work even though at first sight there appear to be rather tenuous links between these different spheres. It is for the reader to explore further by turning to the original sources and forming his own scheme of things.

# 1 Schools, Guidance and Counselling

## THE BACKGROUND TO COUNSELLING

It is generally assumed that the pace of life in western industrial and urban societies has quickened since the Second World War; and that this process continues steadily so that personal adjustments to society, to work, to the family, and to schools become more intense and complex for each succeeding generation. This would inevitably affect the education of young people and expose them to environmental and other problems which can be expected to produce more personal problems in development.

The evidence for this, however, seems slender if we take only the results of surveys made on large numbers of young people. For example, among recent writers who have failed to find such evidence are Fleming (38) and Douglas (27). In the groups of children that Douglas studied there were personality difficulties present in only a small proportion. For his group as a whole there were no severe periods of unsettlement that could be considered characteristic of adolescence. Nor was there any evidence of emotional stress and unbalanced behaviour in the reports of the mothers or teachers. This certainly indicates that adolescents are not in need of psychotherapy on any grand scale. Yet common observation and experience, although a fickle and unreliable guide at times, suggests that it is a very natural thing that many young people, perhaps the majority, at some time or other in their lives should see themselves as having problems and anxieties and should feel the need to discuss these with others. While schools seem to have managed without counsellors so far, it is becoming increasingly difficult to find members of school staffs with the time and the skills to listen sympathetically and who can offer an opportunity to talk through problems unhurriedly, without censure, or judgment.

Moreover, change in society and its effect on schools has been well documented, and this in itself provides evidence of future problems (note 1). An observer from another culture, the American Richard Gross, spent a year in this country observing British education, both state and private. He comments (43, p.547):

> Yet it is clear to any perceptive visitor that Britain is in a state of flux. Great alterations threaten its past-orientated outlook. The end of Empire, the upward surge of the lower classes, the technological revolution, the rise of meritocracy, her role in NATO and the Atlantic Community, the challenge of the Common Market—all these are having numerous repercussions on British life.

The contributions of the twenty-three British educators to Gross's book offered some clues as to what may be the implications for British education. While details and emphasis vary with each writer's prejudices and predilections yet there is some measure of agreement on trends in our present day society. Changes in so many areas of human activity are bound to affect the upbringing and training of children and young people in a variety of ways, known and unknown, direct and indirect. Any discussion of these changes and their likely effects must be speculative, but necessary in order to understand the context in which counselling is being introduced.

A hierarchical structure between members of different classes where each individual's position was fixed and immutable is being replaced by a horizontal network of professional and job inter-connections where vertical mobility between classes is accepted as normal and natural. Although there are many features in society which still appear to emphasise class differences (such as modes of speech, forms of dress, housing and so on) such differences are fast becoming less important. Regional differences also (perhaps because families are geographically more mobile than ever before) seem to be of less significance than formerly. Improved forms of communication with more frequent contacts between people are the most powerful factors here: standardisation of transport, immediacy of verbal communication (telephone, television, radio), together with rising standards of living spread throughout the population.

Contemporary society seems to be changing rapidly from one where the authority connected with obedience to a tradition is disappearing. To be told what to do without questioning is no longer acceptable. The new expectations are based on consultation and participation in decision-making between equals. Each individual is to be respected as a person in his own right, with a right to differ and to belong to a minority whether of race, creed or colour. The old religious traditions are breaking down, uncertainty and doubt replacing the confidence and certainty characteristic of deeply held convictions. Religious and social values, formerly widely acknowledged, are no longer accepted as having universal validity. One of the greatest influences creating what Elvin (29) calls a 'multi-belief' society is a scientific way of thinking. This is expressed succinctly by Wrenn (134, p.13):

> The most pervasive of all perhaps is the scientific mode of thought. All the technological advances that are reshaping the world are based upon the work of investigators whose tools are careful observations, controlled experiments and disciplined thought. But science, of course, is more than technology. The scientist is an adventurer and creator. He searches for truth—the hidden beauty—as does the artist or poet, he pauses to prove them. He thinks in terms of how little we know, not how much. He realises that no generalisation can be drawn from a single incident no matter how dramatic, that probability, not finality, is the ruling law of nature, that 'truth' is a tentative thing.

The breakdown in traditional beliefs and the search for personal significance in a mass society seems to expose everyone to greater insecurity. In Great Britain larger groupings—for example, in local government—are reflected in education by the move to larger educational units such as comprehensive schools. Such groupings, increasing in size for reasons of economy and efficiency, emphasise by contrast the dwindling significance of the individual. It is by no means certain that large comprehensive schools offer the best chance to some children unless at the same time greater emotional support can be ensured for those who need it. Students handicapped by poor homes will not necessarily lose these handicaps when comprehensive education becomes universal. 'Perhaps more rather than less attention will be needed to enable the able boy or girl from a deprived home to use to the full the opportunities offered by his comprehensive school.' (Douglas, 28).

New knowledge is growing so fast that it is becoming increasingly difficult for the educator to keep up-to-date, even in a narrow field. Personal experience of vocational problems, as elsewhere, is often of little help to the present day pupil or student. It has to be expected that, within the next few years new jobs, at present only a dream, will appear. Many jobs now in existence seem likely to vanish. The young person can expect to be re-trained during his working life for at least one change of occupation and such training is likely to be very different from his initial training.

The family has always been known as a potent influence in the development of the individual but it is only recently that changes in family patterns, and in the relationship of the family to community life, have assumed greater importance in schools. The school counsellor must know how families vary and how this variation is related to the social environment (see chapter 6 for an extended discussion on this aspect). The settled, long-established rural community of the last century or the secure patterns of family relationship of such urban communities as the East End of London (Young and Wilmott, 135) offered the emotional support of easily available relatives, friends and neighbours and a range of satisfying social activities whereby a sense of identity and of personal worth was secured.

Now increasing geographical and social mobility has altered this picture. Families can expect to move home several times in a life time and certainly more than once during the formative years of childhood. This means that the members of a community are continually shifting and changing and the community itself is more impersonal and less supportive than formerly, often creating new conditions for producing family insecurity or for exaggerating family instability. Even with relatively stable family patterns, urbanisation and the city life remains dull, limited and unimaginative. It restricts children's personal growth in many ways by offering inadequate outlets for physical and psychological challenge. Attempts to find remedies are continually being made on the lines of, for example, 'Outward Bound',

'Adventure Playgrounds' or Country House Holiday Courses for children. Improved community support is sought for the family as it can easily become psychologically isolated and needs the extended support of anyone, or any organisation, that might help. In this situation the school can be seen as one of the means of family support by their attempt to establish effective communication and to provide a focus for a vigorous, meaningful and constructive community life.

The last few years have seen a succession of national reports (42) in this country on most aspects of education. These reports draw attention to the need for changes in education and for their spread through the national educational system quickly and widely. One of the main characteristics that is emphasised again and again in these reports is the need to pay attention to each individual within the school or university so that waste of talent and ability can be contained, that causes of failure in adjustment to the educational programme can be investigated and some appropriate form of personal help can be offered when needed. Greater consideration must be given to each individual in fostering growth and personal development and in offering wider choices and broader educational opportunities than before. These reports too, reveal many deficiencies in education. For example, there is a failure to develop the ability of large numbers of young people, especially at the secondary level. The reasons, which are numerous, may be related to an unattractive curriculum; or to the absence of help with a personality weakness; or the inability of the school to compensate adequately for domestic, family or social handicaps. It is here that over-large classes and lack of staff point the need for trained counsellors as one way of helping the handicapped young person to integrate within the school.

Partly as a result of these reports, and partly as a result of the mood of the times, when change everywhere is in the air, schools are, and increasingly will be, involved in introducing new methods of education. This has happened fairly extensively in infant and junior schools, and to a lesser extent in the secondary schools. Many of these new educational ideas, spreading upwards to the secondary schools, are already much in evidence and form the background against which an attempt is being made to introduce a more sophisticated and extensive guidance and counselling system into schools. The work of the school counsellor offers a useful complement to these major changes in structure and content.

The introduction of various forms of programmed learning, teaching machines, closed-circuit television and a whole host of audio-visual aids, together with such ideas as integrated curricula in primary schools, vertical or family grouping in infant schools, the move towards extending comprehensive schools, and non-streaming, indicate an increasing rate of change in schools. Such changes themselves produce tensions and anxieties especially if the school staff are not completely in harmony with them. It is important in this situation that school counselling is not seen as a simple method of cushioning the effect of change, as one recent headline in a national educational paper suggests: 'Counsellors demanded after outbreaks of violence'. Such expectations of counselling must lead to disappointment. School counselling is only able to flourish in those schools where there is already a general acceptance amongst the staff of the new approach towards young people and a well developed school counselling system can be one of the supports to aid the teacher through the difficulties of such a transition.

## TEACHING, GUIDANCE AND COUNSELLING

Until very recently the teacher's role has been defined mostly by tradition and is so still in most of our schools. In commenting on secondary schools Gill (41) observes 'Schools remain essentially subject-centred in that members of staff are appointed to teach certain subjects and pupils have time-tables which prescribe the subject studies that will clearly occupy each period'. In spite of the pressures for change, the teacher's main function is still that of an authority on the teaching of a subject. Control and direction appear the main attributes rather than a 'service' function. In Britain in all schools teaching has always had a welfare or pastoral care aspect. Such a dual role is a little difficult to sustain with today's increasing demands on the teacher.

Disciplinary matters, and concern for each student's personal development, need more time, as well as special preparation or training. Hence a school or educational counsellor fits easily into the position of a professional within the school who can usefully complement the class teacher's welfare role and who can offer a psychological service linking the teacher with specialised services outside the school.

The teacher's role with its counselling and pastoral care aspects is not diminished by having specialist counsellors within the school. These aspects will continue, and often may well increase, as additional support is provided by the school counsellor and greater knowledge of the available outside agencies is absorbed and used. It is probably true to say that other professional roles are often easier to define than the teaching role in that it tends to be general rather than specific. Wilson (128) analyses the teacher's role from a sociologist's viewpoint. Whenever personal services are provided it is nearly always difficult to define them briefly and precisely and they seem particularly prone to 'considerable conflicts and insecurities'. If the teacher is to act as a 'socialising agent' and to compensate for home deficiencies, then he must be in a position 'to foster a sustained relationship with the child'. In this sense there are always likely to be counselling aspects to teaching, and M. Argyle (3) suggests that this aspect of counselling is very much the common concern of all. He writes (p.203):

> A person's social competence and general personality development can be assisted if he is given feedback about his shortcomings. This is done on social skill training courses and in psychotherapy. People are often in trouble or distress and in need of help. It has been found that much can be done by people who are untrained and unskilled in psychotherapy, provided they establish a helping relationship. This involves an acceptance of the other, a sympathetic appreciation of his problems, and the provision of a warm and supporting relationship . . . this relationship is not obvious to common sense and goes beyond traditional moral ideas in many ways.

From everyday usage and from earlier comments, it seems that there are common features in the use of the three terms, teaching, guidance and counselling. It is necessary to be clear, however, on the difference of function between the three as only confusion and muddle will result from a failure to distinguish between them. As already stated, the teacher, especially perhaps in secondary schools, is an authority figure who controls and directs the individual in relation to groups. He is the key figure in helping others to acquire knowlege of a subject, or of an area of knowledge mainly concerned with passing examinations. The emphasis is on techniques of learning and while it can be argued that there are other ways of examining based on continuous assessment, yet it is still characteristic of education in this country that one of the main aims is the preparation of students for an examination. Taylor (107, p.38) makes this point unequivocally for the secondary modern schools:

The modern school has made clear the nature and extent of the social pressures at work in this country during the past fifteen years by the way it has largely repudiated its elementary and general aims in favour of work that enables it to contract into the system of examinations, competition and success.

Teachers as a group (although with many exceptions) show certain characteristics inevitably stemming from the nature of the work. Shields (87) puts this point thus: 'Teachers are inclined to be individuals who are accustomed (if not inclined) to direct, command, decree, evade, pontificate, request, ordain, prescribe, impose, bid, enjoin, charge, call upon, instruct, insist, summon, beckon, promulgate, call, send, judge, assess and otherwise decide for others what they ought to do'. Teaching stresses the intellectual and the instructional and requires different attributes from those demanded in counselling where the stress is on feeling. F. Roberts (76) emphasises the point that 'the pedagogic role of the teacher is quite different from, and should not be confused with, the "listening" role of the counsellor'. On the other hand, the apparent conflict between intellectual and emotional education is in many schools becoming much less than formerly. A planned guidance and counselling programme can reduce this conflict even further.

Guidance has been used in several ways in this country. It is well known that 'child guidance' is a term which describes a certain kind of professional approach to children and young people based on the team approach of psychiatrist, educational psychologist and psychiatric social worker. These teams are to be found in child guidance centres or clinics run by local authorities. They are a specialist service available to parents, doctors, teachers and others. Gertrude Kier in her article on the 'history of child guidance' (55) comments:

> Child guidance has been defined as 'giving expert advice or assistance to parents, educationists and to the children themselves, in those individual cases where doubt has arisen about the best way of directing or re-directing the child's mental development'. In this sense the idea of child guidance is at least as old as Plato, and is to be found in various forms in the writings of all educational thinkers—Comenius, Rousseau, Pestalozzi, Froebel. But anything like a scientific approach to the subject was of necessity compelled to wait until scientific methods had been applied to the problems of childhood generally and to those of individual differences.

An equally well known use of the term guidance is vocational guidance, and this use of the term is discussed in more detail in the next chapter. Guidance in this sense studies systematically each school-leaver with a view to suggesting possible careers or jobs. Another use of the term occurs in the phrase educational guidance which is used, for example, by the National Foundation for Educational Research in their handbook on tests, *Educational Guidance in Schools*. Guidance here refers to forms of mental and educational measurement that can be carried out by means of group tests. Such a narrow meaning of the term refers to objective assessments by means of standardised group tests covering educational, personality and intellectual measures. The results have an important function in the assessment of groups and can often be used as a basis for individual interviews. (See note 2).

A much wider definition of guidance was used by the editors of the 1955 *Yearbook of Education* (44) who, after great difficulty in reaching a definition generally acceptable to their contributors, defined guidance as 'a process of helping individuals through their own efforts to discover and develop their potentialities both for personal happiness and social usefulness'. Such a definition is so wide that it would include anything that happens between teacher and taught in education. It could be a definition of education itself. Widening the concept even further Wall (118) would include 'an analysis of the environment in terms of the needs of children; the attempt to determine how these needs may be supplied by the family, by the school, or by some other means and the necessary help to parents and teacher which will help them to discharge their functions'.

There are a number of peculiar difficulties then in defining guidance in order to distinguish it from counselling. The chief difference here lies in the authority of the person doing the guidance. A guidance system in schools is one which implies compulsion; it happens to everyone in a school as everyone is forced by law to attend school. A guidance system in a school involving psychometric assessment implies that everybody within the school must pass through the programme of testing or assessment. Guidance is a systematic way of collecting information about individuals and groups by means of objective and standardised tests. Such information is partly for the use of the school and staff in their attempts to classify and grade individuals. Such assessments may be, but are not necessarily, discussed with individuals. Classifying, grading, advising, recommending, persuading and suggesting are the overall characteristics of decision-making in the guidance field.

Within recent years the term counselling has achieved greater prominence in many different professional fields. The term counsellor was first used in an official educational publication in this country in the Newsom report (42, para.233): 'In large schools it may not be fanciful to look forward to a stage where there is a full-time counsellor available to advise the pupils throughout their school course and to prepare them for going out into the world'. More than thirty years ago there was a Diploma Course at Birmingham University in the Psychology of Counselling. Again counselling is a well known activity of marriage guidance counsellors and the National Marriage Guidance Council has been prominent in this country over a number of years in training counsellors for work in education as well as for individual counselling in marriage breakdown.

Counselling can be defined very widely as any professional activity which makes for good communication between people. Such a broad definition then would include anything that happens between teacher and student, between individual members of a school staff, between parents and schools, that makes for smooth and satisfying personal relationships, and for the easing of tensions or for the formation of a school climate that facilitates learning and personal growth. There is, however, a much narrower definition of counselling which is a technical one and which includes all the common features in counselling used by all the professions, both old and new. Counselling in this sense is a relationship between two people where one person (the client) is aware of a problem and of the need to talk it over with another (the counsellor). The latter is the kind of person who can listen with sensitivity and understanding and who has available a range of skills and knowledge to help over this problem (see chapter 5). In this book the term counselling will be used in this sense, unless indicated otherwise.

Such a narrow definition borders on psychotherapy and introduces many problems of how such counselling might perhaps be implemented in a school setting. It is meant to be available to all children and young people, and is not primarily for those with special handicaps. The latter may be helped by counselling although the techniques and methods used derive more from the study of, and experience with, the normal rather than the abnormal.

## THE SCHOOLS AND COUNSELLING

School counselling as a full-time profession in English schools is only at an early stage although it has been part of the educational scene in Scandinavia and the United States for many years. The total number of school counsellors is still small, although growing rapidly. The newly formed National Association of Educational Counsellors numbered 100 members at the beginning of 1969, most of whom had passed through recognised training courses. The total number of school counsellors in the country, however, is certainly much larger than this, as there are many, both part-time and full-time, who are untrained. There are no national figures at present available of the number of untrained counsellors and the general picture is of great role diversity and uncertainty among the untrained and very uneven development throughout the country. Some of the larger secondary schools (usually with more than 1,500 pupils) have seven or more counsellors, all acting part-time and all untrained.

School counselling practice in other countries and several recent articles on current British practice (see for example Taylor, 105) show that three counselling roles are being developed in this country—the psychometric role, or tester (already performed by some teachers), the therapeutic role or personal counsellor (where the counsellor deals with behaviour problems and other personality difficulties), and the vocational guidance role (already performed in the best schools as a team responsibility between teacher, careers master and Youth Employment Officer). Every counsellor should have some acquaintance with each role although it is doubtful whether all three roles can be carried out expertly enough by one person (see Taylor, 106 and chapter 2 below).

Present British training courses offer a training in this three-fold role and this model is likely to continue for the foreseeable future since it appears to be more immediately adaptable to the needs of British education. The first training courses for school counsellors in British schools started in October 1965 with one-year courses at Keele and Reading Universities. Exeter University followed in 1966, and Swansea University in 1969. These training courses are still at an early stage of development and offer a wide variety of approach and method.

There are advantages in the school counsellor having a general training course covering all three roles as he will then be able to fill any role offered him, by inclination, by preference, or by the needs of the school. The training for the counsellor then should be 'sufficiently flexible to permit his personal feelings and temperamental inclinations to play some part in deciding the style of his preferred role and to allow him some choice in the selection of areas of need to which he may devote his time and energy'. (Daws, 25).

Some role confusion in such a rapidly developing field is inevitable where not only have the schools still to accept the counsellor as an essential part of school life but where there is no agreement as yet on the precise role or roles to be undertaken. It is certain that a school counsellor's role overlaps with many other professional roles such as that of teacher, social worker, educational psychologist, psychiatrist, psychotherapist, and many others. This role uncertainty can create tensions and anxieties that seem to be characteristic of those professions which are closely involved with people. Another reason for tension and anxiety is that new roles evolve or appear and old roles are modified (or sometimes disappear) as a response to newly discovered needs or changes in values (see note 3). The level at which the counsellor uses his particular skills for a particular role may depend on where he sees he can make his most effective contribution in the school, and how the staff and the headmaster wish his role to be defined. Clearly to a large extent the roles of a profession are determined by the nature of the society in which it is practised, but it is not completely satisfactory for the school counsellor's role to be defined from outside.

In personal and therapeutic counselling, specialised training after selection, followed by adequate supervision after training, are essential. Special qualities of personality are necessary before practising this role. This is demonstrated by the marriage guidance movement in this country (see note 4) where rigorous selection is carried out and a high percentage of failures to qualify for the initial training is shown. Many local authorities are developing forms of in-service training in personal relationships. For example, G. Roberts (77) describes an approach which involved very careful selection of teachers who were subsequently trained to carry out forms of personal counselling in Wiltshire schools. Changes in schools or in the climate of opinion have emphasised the present gaps in the provision of adequate guidance and counselling services, highlighting the main requirements. There is a need for continuous assessments covering the whole of school life by objective test programmes as most of our secondary schools do not have a thoroughly planned and co-ordinated testing programme. There is need also for a greater concentration of resources within the school, special services for the delinquent, the emotionally disturbed, and the anti-social. A thorough and systematic scheme of vocational or careers guidance on the lines suggested by Daws (26) is also necessary. (See note 5).

Where the test role or vocational guidance or careers role is being already performed satisfactorily, then obviously the school counsellor role needs to be supporting only and concentration on the therapeutic/personal side becomes possible. F. Roberts (76), working as a counsellor in a large London comprehensive school, concerned himself quite deliberately and specifically with the AFFECTIVE aspects of personality. Such a role for all counsellors is supported elsewhere, e.g. A. W. Rowe (83), the head of a large comprehensive school, suggests that any role other than the personal/therapeutic one would be out of place in his school; on the other hand A. Jones as counsellor at Mayfield Comprehensive School (53) deliberately limited counselling to personal guidance, as vocational guidance proper requires in the counsellor possibly different qualities and a great deal of technical knowledge about job opportunities and qualifications. A different view is proposed by other heads, e.g. Sharp (86) considers that those attributes prominent in personal counselling can best be carried out by the head of a house of 140 children responsible for all aspects of the child's personal welfare. 'The only aspect of counselling which is seen as so specialised as to be handled by one person is careers guidance.'

It is the experience in most schools that a disproportionate amount of time can be spent by staff in trying to handle sympathetically a small number of difficult personality problems. Two or three children, whose greatest need sometimes is for psychological help and understanding, can disrupt class work for long periods. Although one cannot stress a priority need for personal counselling on the basis only of helping the classroom teacher, yet with a suitably trained counsellor some help can be given. For example, F. Roberts (76), as part of a campaign to introduce personal counselling into a London comprehensive school, attempted group counselling with a few boys who were particularly disruptive and aggressive in the classroom. Although the main purpose on this occasion was for the counsellor to be of practical help to the classroom teacher the volunteers for this counselling group met regularly for the discussion of emotional problems. The staff were able to point to the improved work and changed attitude of the boys concerned.

### WHO SHOULD BE COUNSELLED?

There is great variation among young people in the degree to which they appear to need help over personal problems and in the ways they seek that help. Some will prefer to help themselves or will be helped by parents, but spurn opportunities for discussion; some will prefer to be helped by the professional services outside the school or college; others will be helped by relatives, or friends, or a subject teacher. But many young people and children find it hard to communicate effectively with parents, or parent figures, or with people in a position of authority where moral prescription and directives may seem inevitable. Some, even with supporting help from admired adults may find it a confusing, muddling experience to be in the psychological doldrums between childhood dependence and adult independence. 'I am neither/nor. Grown-ups can't treat me as an equal because I'm obviously not a grown-up, and yet I'm still a baby in many ways' was the *cri-de-coeur* of one fourteen-year-old.

There is little objective evidence in this country of the numbers of young people who might benefit from counselling. Clearly the numbers of young people who might avail themselves of a school counsellor is much greater than the numbers who might be considered to be maladjusted; but the incidence of maladjustment in the population offers a minimum estimate of the need for personal counselling. There is a fairly widespread agreement among experts, as Stott (99), that this incidence amongst school children is likely to be about ten per cent although the Underwood report (42) pointed out that there were considerable difficulties in getting any reliable estimate. In the investigation undertaken by this committee the percentages of children deemed maladjusted varied widely in different parts of the country from approximately five per cent to twenty per cent or more. Certainly existing school psychological and child guidance services are unable to deal with a problem of this size, even if these services are expanded rapidly as suggested by both the Underwood report and the Summerfield report (42). It appears essential to consider alternative methods and services.

In an American Junior High School of 780 students, Boy and Pine (12) found that 47 per cent of the student population consulted three full-time counsellors in one year. About a third of the problems dealt with concerned the educational area (curriculum and teaching), just over a half, personal problems and the remainder were vocational and career problems. Although more experience of school counselling is needed in this country before the American figures can be applied in English education yet it indicates quite clearly that the numbers who respond to a counselling programme can be quite large.

The National Marriage Guidance Council has accumulated much evidence of the need to extend their work to schools and colleges. John Wallis, formerly training officer in charge of training counsellors for the NMGC examines in a series of three articles (121, p.165) some of the problems of selection, training, philosophy and recruitment to this new profession.

In the last few years professional people increasingly refer clients to marriage counsellors. Not only that, they themselves turn to the National Marriage Guidance Council for knowledge of marriage counselling and for training in it. The National Marriage Guidance Council and local Marriage Guidance Councils are frequently approached by professional people (both individually and in groups) for training in marriage or educational counselling—by doctors, clergy, teachers, health visitors, welfare officers, prison and Borstal staff, youth workers and solicitors. We do little to answer their requests and nothing at all to provide any systematic, generic training in . . . counselling for members of the professions.

Many local authorities have collaborated closely with the NMGC in developing forms of counselling in schools (see Stuart, 100), for one easily accessible account. Here the problem was seen as discovering teachers who could be specially selected for in-service training in personal relationships. On return to their schools these teachers would be available for personal counselling within the school. The aim was to enable the teachers 'to establish an understanding with their pupils so that in discussion the pupils can themselves find an answer to some of their problems in the field of personal relationships'. Many teachers agreed that there existed in schools a need for individual personal counselling and that special resources of time, space and money were needed to develop such a service.

## COUNSELLING AND MENTAL HEALTH

The belief is widely held that education must seek to improve mental health. For Jahoda (52) the idea of a mentally healthy person is indeed a vague one, and no agreement is possible on definitions. But as with definitions of counselling, it is not necessary to agree on definitions of mental health before embarking on programmes of prevention or treatment, or before attempting to identify people who may be 'at risk'. Jahoda considers mental health either as a relatively constant and lasting attribute of personality or as a momentary function of different situations. A mentally healthy person can be one who has a positive and realistic attitude towards himself and others and who is able to distinguish reality and phantasy. He is able to take life as it comes and to achieve mastery over it. He can accept the discrepancy between the 'ideal' self and the 'real' self to achieve a satisfying identity. He demonstrates concern for others, has a unifying philosophy and is able to work for long-range goals. The mentally unhealthy person has difficulties in all these areas.

A rigorous analysis of concepts of moral education, normality and maladjustment is attempted by Wilson (129) who concludes that everyone is at some stage in their development 'substantially below par in their mental health'. A well recognised task of the teacher is to identify students with mental health problems. One guide, admittedly arbitrary, is to equate mental ill-health with the behaviour shown by the disturbed or maladjusted personality. Many problems arise in the identification of mentally unhealthy people, but it is likely that where the school staff can exchange views easily among themselves they are more likely to be sensitive to the difficulties of individual pupils. A whole range of professional social services, health visitors, pre-school play groups, nursery classes and schools, infant-welfare clinics, the school medical service, child guidance clinics, general practitioners and so on are involved outside the schools—and increasingly so—in the detection and prevention of mental ill-health. It is impossible to say with any precision how effective this preventive work can be in the absence of controlled investigations. Everyone has a responsibility for being ready to help others who might be at risk, or to suggest people or services who might be capable of offering help, although there are always likely to be some mental health problems that escape detection. Some parents or families refuse help or will not recognise the need of it. Professional vigilance varies and occasionally the obvious will be missed by even the most skilled.

Some mental health problems subside while others only declare themselves in response to a new or changed situation. The school counsellor is one more additional aid supplementing the teacher's observations, and can often help to deal with minor problems within the school setting, acting as a screen for reference to specialist services elsewhere. Crises in personal development frequently occur in the school—playing truant, refusing school, tensions within the family causing (temporary) upset, involvement with the police, extremely low achievement, these and many other problems will be an indication of personality difficulty that may need the aid of the counsellor.

## THE EFFECTIVENESS OF COUNSELLING PROCEDURES

Whenever any systematic attempt is made to apply scientific methods to behaviour, objective methods are necessary to determine the effectiveness of the means used. Even when a specialist team of investigators, uninvolved in the day-to-day situation, appraises the situation objectively to get at the facts, the results are seldom dramatic and unequivocal. There may be gaps in experimental design or some inability to control all the variables, and varying interpretations of the results are possible. When studies have been made of the effectiveness of counselling procedures, claims can be made which are not always justified by the evidence offered, and little agreement exists amongst experts as to how research findings might be used or interpreted. Research must be interpreted with caution yet must also be recognised as an essential feature on which some facts can be used as a possible basis to guide and to alter practice. It is not possible to give a definite answer to the question: how effective are counselling procedures? Neither is there agreement on whether the attempts to measure the success of counselling have any meaning. The most that can be claimed is that there is no evidence to suggest that counselling procedures do not lead to significant attitude change on the part of the person being counselled.

It is not possible here to present a balanced survey of the various investigations, mostly American, into counselling effectiveness but the study by Shouksmith and Taylor (88) is offered as an example of the methodological problems involved with an outcome favourable to counselling. They selected three groups of high ability but low-achievement children, aged twelve to thirteen years, from a New Zealand intermediate school. The kind of counselling given was non-directive and was based on a listening-caring-helping relationship between teacher and child. It was felt that such a relationship, offered by the teacher who was not emotionally involved in the child's problems, might lead to the child wanting to work for the teacher, and hence the child would improve in attainments. In this way the hypothesis was tested that a short period of regular counselling would help children of high intelligence to overcome some personal problems affecting their academic work.

> The counselling technique used was made as simple as possible so that if the method proved successful it could readily be used by general teachers without a long period of training in counselling. Counselling was generally non-directive as the counsellor acted as a sounding board for the child's problems, a sympathetic listener who showed a personal interest, who encouraged the subject to seek his own solutions and who offered suggestions only when an impasse seemed to have been reached and help was sought. Shouksmith and Taylor (88).

The authors concluded from this study that 'counselling does have a positive effect on under-achieving pupils' and such conclusions appear on the surface to be justified by the evidence offered. Unfortunately, because of weakness in the design of this study, there is no certainty that the counselling of the children was the only factor making for improvement as the number of variables left uncontrolled was very great. For example, parents were interviewed in the experimental group (some on many occasions) but not in the other two groups. Such improvement in achievement could have been due to many other causes. The greater involvement of the parents in the experimental group may have induced attitude changes in the children. The duration of the experiment was limited by practical necessity and it was felt that 'a longer period of counselling might well have produced greater improvements', but there cannot, of course, be any certainty of this. In spite of methodological difficulties in experimental design (most of which are recognised by the authors) it was concluded that: 'From the practical standpoint, the results of this experiment suggest that the present school programme should be extended to include counselling with under-achieving pupils, particularly those of high ability'. (See note 6.)

## SUMMARY

Changes in society, in family life and in schools create conditions where greater attention to individual needs is necessary. Counselling is one of the ways in which this attention can be developed.

Counselling, however, needs to be distinguished from both teaching and guidance in spite of the overlapping function of each of these areas. Counselling is one part of the overall guidance process and deals mainly with the emotional side of development. It differs, too, from both guidance and teaching by trying to be less authoritarian and non-censorious in approach to the individual.

Counselling is not new, but school counsellors are newcomers to English education and have yet to establish themselves in any numbers in English schools. There is no agreement in these early stages as to the roles that will be adopted. The counsellor's tasks overlap with those of many other professionals—teachers, social workers, educational psychologists, psychiatrists and probation officers. Training courses already established in several universities attempt to train for a composite of skills so that counsellors can trim their sails according to the wind.

It is suggested that the primary role of the school counsellor is to be readily available in schools, both primary and secondary, so that every young person in difficulty is helped. Subsidiary roles will include being an expert in devising psychometric programmes of assessment and in careers and vocational guidance.

Counselling is an activity practised by many professions, both old and new, which demands training and a rather special attitude. Teaching has counselling aspects and these can be developed by appropriate in-service training.

The school counsellor draws on many disciplines to provide the theoretical background to his work and he will use the result of research in many related fields to widen his knowledge and sharpen his perceptions. He will be aware of the limitations of his role and will be ready to be flexible and adaptable in this pioneering situation. It is better to concentrate on the quality of counselling than to attempt to cope with large numbers.

## NOTES

1. See for example Vaizey (110), Bantock (5), Elvin (29). For a recent American view see Wrenn (134). M. Kellmer Pringle *Investment in Children* (Longmans 1966) is relevant to many of the points in the early part of this chapter.

2. If individual psychometric assessments are needed in this country this can only be done by professionally recognised clinical or educational psychologists; and further information about this can be obtained from the British Psychological Society (13). Alternatively, the local educational psychologist can be consulted.

3. This is particularly noticeable in the newer professions such as child guidance work. Lees (61) describes a situation in one local authority area where roles of PSW, EWO, CCO (see p.45), are changing partly as a response to social pressures and social needs. The PSW is beginning to make contact with many other social workers in the field acting as a consultant rather than in a narrow treatment role as in the past. An extension of the traditional teacher's functions to include social and welfare work has been suggested by M. Craft (chapter 14, 'The teacher/social worker' in Craft, Rayner & Cohen (23)). Drastic changes in the EWO's role are suggested by T. Hughes in *Association of Educational Psychologists Newsletter*, Spring, 1967, in an article entitled 'Changes envisaged in the Educational Welfare Service'.

4. The National Marriage Guidance Council has local branches and is a voluntary organisation that helps with marriage difficulties. The marriage guidance counsellors are voluntary part-time social workers and at their best offer a service of high quality personal counselling. Recently educational and preventive work has been developed and often schools have called on the services of these counsellors to an increasing extent as part of their personal relationships programme. (See Wallis 121, 122.)

5. A survey conducted in 1964 by the Careers Research and Advisory Centre (CRAC), an independent organisation, showed that just over half of the 224 schools involved had careers masters (cf. A. G. Watts, Educational Director of CRAC addressing the Arnold Society at Cambridge and reported in the *Times Educational Supplement* of 5 March, 1965. Even in those schools where there is a careers teacher there are problems associated with lack of facilities, training and time. Also cf. pp.79-80 Carter (17).)

6. The child of high ability (the gifted child) can sometimes raise special problems within a school. How these might be partially resolved is suggested in J. B. Shields *The Gifted Child* (NFER 1968).

## FURTHER READING

There are no textbooks written for school counsellors in British schools at the time of writing. Holden (48) describes personal counselling from the point of view of the practising teacher who does part-time counselling. There are several publications and articles which give some information about the current situation in counselling in this country. Foremost among these is the Schools Council Publication on *School Counselling* (22) and the National Association for Mental Health Publication (ed. by Grace Rawlings, 1969) on *School Counselling*. Wallis (122) describes the principles and practice of counselling which has relevance to other fields as well as to marriage guidance.

Hughes' article (50) gives a useful description of recent thinking relating guidance and counselling concepts to the British scene.

Hall and Lauwerys (Eds.) (44) devote a complete issue of the *Yearbook of Education*, to European guidance services, much of which is relevant to recent practice and developments in school counselling.

The American literature in guidance and counselling is vast and uneven in quality. The first and most comprehensive bibliography on the American literature on counselling is to be found in (40). Probably the best introductions to the American field are to be found in Boy and Pine (12), Stewart and Warnath (95), and Wrenn (134). Lytton (65) give a recent British view of American school counselling after a period of observation in the United States. There are recently-published articles to be found in such journals as *New Era* and *Marriage Guidance*.

Two recently published books offering extensive bibliographies are: Anne Jones *School Counselling in Practice* (Ward Lock Educational 1970); Ethel Venables *Counselling* (National Marriage Guidance Council 1970).

# 2 The Counsellor Inside and Outside the School

## SOME DIFFICULTIES IN SCHOOL COUNSELLING

Schools are no longer considered to be autonomous communities unrelated to what goes on outside their boundaries. Although the learning of subjects is still one of their most important tasks schools are no longer seen as hot-houses for forcing growing minds into pre-determined patterns. Before a start is made to educate, the assumptions the educator now makes are different from those made in the past. He first considers the differences between individuals in special abilities, in personality and temperament, in drive to achieve, in home background, in social and emotional history, in needs and in interest. Such differences, however we organise education, are the bases from which education must begin. Schools can be seen as very powerful instruments for aiding each person's pattern of growth towards adulthood and maturity. The conscious aim is to plan the school environment to ensure that such personal growth is possible for each individual. School in this sense, then, becomes one of the main agencies helping individuals to relate the ideas they have of themselves to what others think of them and to relate such self-images to the family and to the larger groups outside the family.

The assumptions made in counselling are those behind all education. The axiom that each individual is of supreme worth in and for himself is sometimes difficult to apply when a pupil is a severe management problem in a school, often with a disruptive effect on other children. The needs of the group may sometimes inevitably take precedence over the needs of the individual. Moreover, that each individual is capable of self-direction and choice is an assumption often difficult to apply in those situations when firm direction is necessary, when the safety of the individual, or of others, is at issue, or when the individual's personality is such that rigid boundaries to disturbed behaviour need to be drawn. This occurs sometimes with certain individuals who seem unable to respond to a permissive or understanding attitude without interpreting it as weakness.

A guidance and counselling service in a school probably flourishes best in those schools where the quality of personal relationships among staff, and between staff and students, is already of a high order. A school counsellor is no substitute for general defects in school organisation, or where poor and inadequate communication is a mark of the school's approach to personal relationships. It has to be realised, however, that there are many human problems that will continue to prove intractable and unmodifiable since the knowledge or skills are just not available to deal with them satisfactorily. Many management problems will prove resistant to influence, and many young people of difficult personality will prove beyond help—certainly by the usual counselling approach.

A school counsellor should resist the temptation to cover such a wide field of work (school records, staff discussions, group discussions, devising test programmes, careers as well as personal counselling) that no one area will be covered fully. To cover a broad field superficially is less effective than to cover a narrow field in depth. Since personal and therapeutic counselling demands a special attitude and skill the counsellor needs to be aware of his limitations and to know when to refer to specialist services outside the school. It is easy to get out of depth once psychological helping processes are started. The dilemmas arising here have been outlined by Caspari (19) where she defines counselling as follows: 'In general terms "counselling" might be described as a dialogue between someone with a problem and someone with specialised knowledge who can help in the understanding of the problem'. The timing and nature of interventions in others' problems is a delicate matter involving ethical considerations and the varying definitions of what might constitute a problem, or who is best able to deal with it. It is often difficult to give psychological help to someone who is unaware that help is needed. Many young people may not wish to be involved with the school staff or the school counsellor. Some may not 'take to' the school counsellor; some may feel that their confidence cannot be respected within the school setting and considerable support and respect for this attitude is necessary when it appears.

### COMMUNICATION PROBLEMS BETWEEN STAFF AND COUNSELLOR

Before a school counsellor is appointed, the Head and school staff will be aware of the gaps in providing for pupil needs and how these may best be filled. To this extent steps will already have been taken to try to define the school counsellor's role before his appearance in the school; a role which will complement the staff's role and will be seen as one more professional in the whole network of care and concern for children and young people making for effective personal relationships. If pastoral care is a well-developed function of the staff's role, then this will still continue. Some children and young people will prefer to make the housemaster or a class or subject teacher their personal confidant rather than the school counsellor and this must be respected and supported. Caspari (19) has indicated how important it is to concentrate on increasing the skills of teaching staff in counselling and to be aware of the indirect influence of the curriculum in helping children's emotional problems. If the school is already committed to an educational guidance and teaching programme, all the other aspects of counselling can be dove-tailed in to form a more comprehensive system of guidance and counselling. If there is a well-developed system of careers guidance, then the counsellor's skill in personal counselling can reinforce the treatment of the many personal problems arising from a consideration of careers.

There will be times, as already stated, when the welfare of the majority seems as though it must take precedence over the individual's welfare, and the Head of the school will remain the final arbiter on delicate matters of choice between the welfare of the group and the welfare of the individual. This should offer no significant problems if all staff remain in easy, free and continuous contact, and all have the aim of keeping lines of communication open.

The case conference method in approaching the co-ordination of different specialists and professions can become one of the more effective ways of establishing and maintaining effective communication between counsellor and staff. Other ways will include forms of organisation already well developed in schools such as staff meetings where school policy and administration are discussed, and the frequent informal contacts between staff on a one-to-one basis where specific problems are discussed between counsellor and teacher. The case conference approach is a regular means of discussing problem children in the school with relevant members of staff, in a small committee of people with varied skills and experiences. It is a way, too, of discussing general points in the establishment and the maintenance of a guidance and counselling system within that system. In this way, staff needs for involvement, participation and for information can be satisfied. This is balanced by the counsellor's needs to find out how he is able to help the staff in their day-to-day problems or contribute more effectively to the counselling programme. In this way, too, each can be exposed to the difficulties and tensions of the other and a sharing of skills and responsibility as a basis for planning and action can take place. A delicate task for the counsellor, as well as for each member of staff, is the maintenance of a neutral role and the avoidance of taking sides with the Head against the staff or with the staff against the Head.

Respect for, and toleration of, differences of skill and attitude is the core of good communication. The notion that good communication can come about merely by offering more and better information is fallacious—it will inevitably be interpreted in different ways by different people; this is particularly relevant, for example, to sex education in schools (see chapter 3). The emotional side of these conferences can also be important. Reasons for breakdown in communication can be explored, tensions, hostilities and anxieties can be released and the need for changes of attitude discussed. Although this is rarer than is often supposed, when good communication is established people respond to each other without feeling threatened or being anxious, in an atmosphere of trust, warmth and acceptance.

What are the likely reasons for breakdown in good communication? These may lie within the counsellor, or within other members of the group. The counsellor may fail to take the lead in trying to develop effective communication or in maintaining personal contacts. He may not make sufficient allowance for the wide variations in personality and temperament in others or for differences in others' values. In short, the counsellor may fail to apply the principles of counselling learned in a one-to-one situation to relationships outside counselling. With the teacher, breakdown may occur on all these points, also, and in a failure to appreciate that smooth progress, co-operation and good communication depends partly on 'give and take', on understanding different viewpoints, in tolerating differeneces in means to achieve agreed aims—the agreed aim being always the welfare of the child or young person. Ambiguities of language can impede understanding. These can occur non-verbally as well as in spoken language—facial and postural language can often reveal attitudes and feelings and, like words, are open to similar misinterpretation. Breakdown may occur in a group through failure to realise what is happening in the group on an emotional level. To know the reasons for a group's mal-functioning may lead to understanding and to effective ways of containing aggressive and hostile feelings.

Stewart and Warnath (95) analyse the many factors making for smooth and easy communication in staff relationships. They suggest several 'barriers to effective communication'. They point to a hierarchical status system amongst teachers, every school staff displaying an often implicit organisation of status levels. One or two teachers may be the largely unacknowledged leaders for the rest of the staff. For example, the younger or more recently qualified may defer to the older, the women to the men, the less experienced to the more experienced. Some staff may possess feelings of insecurity or inadequacy—the nervous, those lacking in confidence, or the apparently less articulate may prefer to conform or to be content without comment or involvement, with others' leadership. A 'natural tendency to judge or evaluate' another person's ideas can lead to the feeling of not being understood, inhibiting any further contributions from the person or persons being judged. There can be no certainty that those attending staff conferences have any desire to learn or are genuinely indifferent—in either case close involvement or participation may be minimal. A resistance to change in one's own attitude or in well established habit systems may well be interpreted as 'defensiveness about the status quo . . . for those who are comfortable about the status quo any change is a threat'. An inability to accept change can often be related in some ways to a lack of personal security. Rigid qualities of thinking and inflexible attitudes can determine some reactions to any discussion of guidance and counselling programmes. There are those who will already know the answers and who are keen to axe discussion. Prejudices are revealed, issues pre-judged and resistances are built up against new learning. Cliques and sub-groups operate in a system of 'inter-personal rivalries'. When this happens the topics for discussion may become only an outlet for such personal rivalries. Lastly, the counsellor may become the focus of aggressive and hostile feelings displaced from other areas or people. 'If some teachers suspect the counsellor of being aligned with the administration, he may also be subject to the fears and hostilities of those who hold these feelings towards administrators.'

In any staff discussion there are at least two levels of communication; the first is easily appreciated as it is the stated purpose of the group's existence in the first place. Fewer people are aware of the existence of a second level; it is certainly less easily noticed as it often exists below the conscious level. Matters will arise that involve personal reactions and below-the-surface feelings. (Stewart and Warnath (95) describe these as 'hidden agendas'). An effective group 'will be aware of the presence of hidden agendas and find ways of coping with them. A group that ignores the personal feelings of a member that may irrationally affect his verbal contributions to a topic under discussion, risks a loss in productivity, a loss of the member'; and 'the group members need to be aware of the possible motives for their action so that they can differentiate between rational differences of opinion and irrational responses unrelated to the topic under discussion'. Any group discussion between counsellor and staff must take into account irrational feelings and ideas—the emotional undertones of the group—if effective communication is to be established.

## VOCATIONAL COUNSELLING AND THE CAREERS ADVISER

Historically, vocational counselling has its roots in vocational guidance. The latter was an attempt to bring a scientific approach to bear on problems of vocational choice by collecting information about an individual from many sources, the home (parents), the school (teachers) and from the objective assessment of abilities, interests and aptitudes. From the data so obtained, the hope was that a sound and reliable basis for guiding the individual to a satisfactory occupation could be achieved. The ultimate aim was to match the intellectual, educational and personality characteristics of an individual with the characteristics known to determine success in particular careers and jobs. Most of the valuable developments in vocational guidance occurred before 1937 with its beginnings stretching back to the earliest years of this century. Many strong influences converged to produce this model or pattern—a reaction against the less desirable influences of the industrial revolution when the human factor seemed to count for little; a growing awareness of the need to provide equal educational and occupational opportunity for all; the existence of misfits and consequent unhappiness in work; the rapidly growing complexity and range of new jobs and the greater skill and training necessary for them.

The drift of the population from the countryside to the town with the resulting concentration of large populations in urban complexities and the decline in family tradition as a basis for choosing a career were two more powerful factors. Such social pressures were linked with the growth of knowledge of the human factor emerging from scientific investigations in industrial psychology, and produced a need for expert professional help for the young school leaver in schools. The scientific analysis of occupational skills and the systematic investigations into methods of work (e.g. time and motion study by which it was found that more efficient ways of carrying out many skills or work tasks could be arrived at by job analysis) produced a body of knowledge which could be used to emphasise the importance of the human factor. More careful selection was seen to be important for many jobs and occupations. Planned, systematic, co-ordinated training programmes were obviously as necessary as satisfying and stable relationships in groups, and adequate financial rewards, in ensuring efficient work practice.

The present Youth Employment Service (or Careers Guidance Service) was developed to help the school leaver in vocational guidance. Since the 1920's the National Institute of Industrial Psychology (NIIP) has provided a systematic vocational guidance service for individuals as well as for schools. One of the foremost exponents in the country on vocational guidance was Professor Alec Rodger (78) who demonstrated the value of such guidance based on precise information about the school leaver (particularly psychometric information), and underlined the need for clearer and more intensive knowledge of occupations. Rodger devoted much time, energy and skill not only to expounding the principles behind successful vocational guidance, but also to offering training to teachers and others through a variety of courses and to encouraging the development of adequate careers guidance in the Youth Employment Service. Although the Youth Employment Service does offer vocational guidance as part of its service, it does not always offer the quality of service that was advocated by Rodger.

Successful vocational guidance work depends on an accurate and full description of the assets of a young person, and wide knowledge of occupations and careers. The first is built up on the continuous assessment of young people by their teachers over a number of years, the result of standardised tests, detailed knowledge of the home background and personal history obtained from the parents. The second is available from many sources, careers handbooks, pamphlets, direct contact with employers' organisations and so on. (See Appendix A for a summary of these). Although Rodger (78) outlined his suggestions for a planned programme of careers guidance over thirty years ago, they are still relevant to much career planning in schools. He suggests that the teachers' function in such guidance should cover the following areas:

1. disseminating information about occupational requirements and opportunities (by, for example, providing relevant books, periodicals, pamphlets, private talks, lectures, film shows, group discussions, and group visits to places of employment, and by acting as an agent for the official and unofficial organisations which undertake to supply news on these matters);
2. collecting data (by interviews and written reports) from parents, doctors and colleagues about boys and girls seeking advice;
3. adding to this data (by making sensible use of tests for general intelligence and special aptitudes, and by planned interviewing);
4. interpreting all the data available in the light of his general knowledge of occupational requirements and opportunities;
5. co-operating with placement organisations in their task of making specific suggestions and finding suitable openings (and, when and where necessary, undertaking this task himself);
6. instructing young people in appropriate methods of applying for posts; and
7. following-up those he advises (by obtaining regular progress reports on their satisfaction and, if possible, on their satisfactoriness).

This is a formidable list of duties indeed.

To help the teacher in his careers work Rodger (78) suggested guides to action in a plan of attack and this might be based on the well known NIIP 7-Point Plan which is still used by psychologists, careers teachers, youth employment officers and others in their careers work. The object of the plan is to make sure that no relevant information is missed and that particular aspects are neither over-stressed nor under-stressed. The Plan can also be used as a basis for analysing job or profession requirements systematically. It is simple to use and its effectiveness for clients may well stem from its being constructed out of an analysis of reasons for failure in occupations so that the client can avoid such pitfalls. The main outline of the Plan is as follows:

*NIIP 7-Point Plan*

1. Circumstances (financial, social, geographical, etc.);
2. physical characteristics (especially disabilities of occupational significance, and such semi-physical characteristics as smartness of bearing, attractiveness of appearance, neatness of dress and pleasantness of voice);
3. attainments (particularly in work, games and other leisure activities);
4. general intelligence;
5. special aptitudes (such as mechanical aptitude, manual dexterity, and aptitudes for drawing and music);
6. interests (especially in intellectual activities, practical and social activities); and
7. disposition (particularly as shown in attitude towards self, towards others, and towards work).

It was the complexity of the whole process of vocational guidance that led Daws to advocate a team approach to vocational guidance as it seemed only reasonable to expect that only by this means 'can the variety of skills and amount of sheer knowledge' (Daws, 26) be made available for a service of high quality. The basic team would be the careers teacher/youth employment officer to which must be added the school counsellor and the social worker (if available) together with other members of staff where relevant (housemaster, tutor, form teacher, etc.). It needs to be continually held in mind that much reliable information is still not available about the reasons for satisfaction or frustration in many occupations. New jobs are appearing, old ones disappearing, job or occupation requirements can change rapidly and most people now can look forward to changing their occupation at least once—perhaps many times in a lifetime.

In the past, careers or vocational guidance tended to be a service offered to the client or school leaver at one particular point in time—when about to leave school, or just before the occupational choice became necessary. It is now seen, however, that such guidance comes too little and too late. By the end of school life future careers have already been determined in many cases by influences outside the school—by peer-group influences, by local availability of occupations and by the family and student as well as by influences within the school. Educational programmes have already been completed and for school leavers at fifteen (to be sixteen by 1973) the areas of educational choice are fairly fixed and limited.

A closer and earlier association of careers guidance with the normal curriculum means a longer, less hurried and less superficial approach than is usual at present. This can mean an increase in the range and extent of choice points and alternatives during a school career. Careers guidance can then be thought of as inseparable from personal development and educational guidance. Veness (111) who carried out a factual survey of school leavers in the London area in 1956 advocated 'an integrated guidance service, covering all facets of the individual and which should be at hand for every school leaver and young adolescent'. It always has been the case that the wise parent and the farsighted teacher have associated vocational opportunity with educational achievement—certain educational paths lead clearly to certain occupational goals. A suitable long-term aim for careers guidance is 'planned procrastination'—a developmental approach to careers where the child is helped throughout his secondary education, over a number of years, to plan his vocational and educational progress. The very process of continuous and extensive guidance becomes the important consideration rather than the outcome. Daws (26) discusses at length Super's contribution to vocational guidance ideas by arguing that 'the school leaver, when choosing an occupation, is seeking to implement a self-concept, and that all the processes of his development are focused upon defining a realistic answer to the question: what sort of person do I wish to become'.

It seems a short step here to see the relevance of Rodger's views on vocational choice (78, see chapter 2); for example, the importance for personal growth, of having time to work through a problem, perhaps over many years, to seek and define a self-image without others intervening too closely or making the decisions. Attempts by others at over-control of vocational goals is not always a sound preparation for adult independence, especially for the older children and young people, as it can reinforce dependency feelings or delay maturity. But for most young people some form of sampling of work is possible: sometimes haphazardly and in unsystematic form such as a paper round, or other form of weekend job, paid or unpaid: sometimes in a planned form when school is used as a base to start the gradual progression from school to work. In this way, too, an abrupt change can often be avoided, and continued support over possible work difficulties can be given. To lose at once all the significant personal relationships from school can prove traumatic for some young people. This can be especially so for those, small in number, who still need a continuing relationship with an adult on leaving school.

## THE COUNSELLOR OUTSIDE THE SCHOOL

Ideally a school counsellor should work closely with a school social worker who would preferably be one of the professionals with direct links to outside agencies. Occasionally the Head or deputy Head of a secondary school performs this function. It is likely, however, that the counsellor himself may have to create many of the links between school and outside agencies and it is important that he should know about them and, if possible, make personal contacts. How these links may be created, and the form they may take, are best dealt with in counsellor training courses rather than in detail here. The list of such contacts is an impressive one. Probation officer (PO), Youth Employment officer (YEO), Citizen's Advice Bureau (CAB), Schools Psychological Service (Educational Psychologist), Education Welfare officer (EWO), different forms of social worker, Psychiatric Social worker (PSW), Child Care officer (CCO), Medical Social worker (MSW), School Medical officer (SMO), health visitor, general practitioner (GP), local Youth Leaders, and Further Education principals. It is impossible here to describe all of these in detail and only those will be selected that seem to be the most relevant for the counsellor. Always, however, the most effective way of finding out about others' roles is by direct contact.

*The Youth Employment Service*

This service is still a young one which came into being with the Employment and Training Act of 1948 (the forerunners of the Youth Employment Service were the Ministry of Labour Juvenile Employment Bureaux dating from 1909). By this Act it became a statutory obligation to provide a form of careers guidance for school leavers. Other statutory duties were (*a*) to help young people to find employment and employers to find suitable workers; (*b*) to provide up-to-date information about occupations and careers for parents and schools, as well as young people, and (*c*) to carry out a follow-up of young people in employment and, if it is needed, to provide further help and guidance. The 1948 Act required every school to register its pupils before leaving school and if local authorities were not operating a Juvenile Employment Service they could start one up. Some local authorities preferred not to do so and hence the Ministry of Labour carried on operating the Youth Employment Service. The overall responsibility at the national level was, however, operated by the Ministry of Labour (now the Department of Employment and Productivity) through the National Youth Employment Council and not by the Department of Education and Science. At the present moment about four-fifths of the service is being run by local education authorities while about one-fifth is administered by the Department of Employment and Productivity.

The functions of Youth Employment officers (sometimes re-named Careers, or Careers Guidance, officers) seem to be determined by two different conceptions of their work. One view of the service's main role is that it is primarily a careers advice and counselling service which should be based clearly on the schools, linking secondary and further education by a common responsibility with teachers for vocational and educational guidance. The other view is that the service should be based on commerce and industry, linking closely with employment and economic planning. In this way it is hoped that the re-training of adults and the re-allocation of workers to different jobs could be more sensitively responsive to rapid technological change.

Carter (17) outlines some of the deficiencies in the present Youth Employment Service. An earlier and higher quality involvement in the school needs to be made, perhaps with advisory work with the school staff. At present not enough time can be given to individual interviews or for the details of the NIIP seven-point plan to be worked out thoroughly. Carter outlines a strong case for re-appraising the scope and role of the service and suggests closer co-operation between the Youth Service and the Youth Employment Service. Daws (26) suggests relieving Youth Employment officers of placement responsibilities as the dual role of being responsible for both placement and guidance 'produces a pre-occupation with assets rather than needs'. This may indicate a future development in careers guidance. One Youth Employment officer would be based completely on the school (a Vocational Guidance officer) while a Youth Employment officer outside the school would concentrate entirely on placement and contact with employers.

*The Social Worker*

There is no generally acceptable definition of a social worker that would cover all the varieties of social work that are in existence. Social workers operate at varying levels of skill from the untrained, unqualified, to the highly qualified graduate with post-graduate training in advanced social work. The setting in which social workers operate varies greatly from a multiplicity of voluntary social agencies in the community—e.g. diocesan moral welfare organisations, the National Society for the Prevention of Cruelty to Children (NSPCC), Care Committees (voluntary social workers attached to schools in the London area (ILEA) and statutory departments such as Child Care. Social workers are trained to work within the limits set by a service or an agency and by using common principles in social work derived from their training. Untrained, unselected voluntary social workers raise special problems as they vary enormously in the help they can offer. At their best they may be able to give sustained and meaningful emotional support to a large number of families in distress. (See note 1.)

The beginnings of a school-based social work service are everywhere apparent (see for example Pedley, 71). Present social work services cannot deal with the large numbers of families that need their help and many of the services that can offer help are turned aside for irrational reasons. For example, a social work setting in a Child Guidance clinic may not be acceptable to some parents because it is a psychiatric clinic: they might prefer to have help through a hospital. While it is true that some parents reject the school setting for equally irrational reasons, many will prefer it. In this way social work based on the school may be able to reach some families resistant to all other social work agencies. The Seebohm report (42) recommended the setting-up of a single social work department, embracing all aspects of social work, for each local authority. This was implemented in the Social Services Act, 1970, and it seems likely that schools will become increasingly associated with these new departments. The first one year training for school social workers was started in the Guidance Unit, Institute of Education, Reading University, in 1967. Such a training is suitable for the social worker who will be attached to a large school, a group of schools, an education department or to the school psychological service of a local education authority. Another variation on this theme is the course for teacher/social workers at Edgehill College of Education, Ormskirk, Lancs., for promoting effectiveness and efficiency. A. W. Wimble (23) elaborates the dangers of confusing the teacher's and social worker's roles.

In a conflict of loyalties the teacher would have to consider the whole school before the individual child and the teacher holds a position of authority. The social worker—professional or voluntary—whilst guiding or advising has always to accept people as they are, and within their own limitations, and moreover she must respect her clients' confidences as does the doctor those of his patients. Parents could properly resent teachers visiting their homes as of right; they might regard it as an intrusion and promptly build up a barricade as a defence. Many children, too, would resent their teachers seeing the poverty or other limitations of their home and getting too close a picture of the ineffectualness of their 'Mum'. The average mother's great need is someone that she can just talk to about her problems . . . they talk much more easily in their own homes to someone who has no authoritative position.

Every local authority appoints Educational Welfare officers (EWO) (formerly known as 'the School Board man' or the School Attendance officer) whose duties in State schools in the past have been connected with ensuring the compulsory attendance of children at school (chasing up the truants) and in being available to help to carry out the numerous statutory social welfare duties that every local education authority must perform—such as arranging transport for children in boarding schools or in special schools. Many of these routine duties will continue. Another role is being suggested for the Education Welfare officer—that of social caseworker who would deal with more complex and difficult family problems than is possible at the moment. The full training would cover three years; a two-year basic course followed by a further year of specialisation. Raising entry requirements and providing high standards of training (mostly based on social case-work principles) will heighten the future effectiveness of the Education Welfare officer and lead to a radical change in education welfare work. It is becoming increasingly the practice to attach an EWO to a school or group of schools with a growing commitment to a social worker's role. Some authorities have combined to produce a form of in-service training while in others a beginning is made to integrate the EWO with the social work in a Child Guidance clinic and Children's department by regular staff conferences (see, for example, Lees (61) who describes such a scheme in operation in Hounslow).

The Psychiatric Social worker (PSW) is a social worker who works mostly in Child Guidance centres or clinics or psychiatric units of large hospitals, although occasionally he works for schools for maladjusted and delinquent children, for voluntary organisations or in local health authorities' community care services. The academic background of the PSW consists of a social science diploma or degree followed by a year's specialised training in a university (several universities run such training courses, e.g. Leeds, Manchester, London, etc.). They are trained to assist families in crisis or breakdown, often in a psychiatric setting and are widely recognised as highly skilled caseworkers. They help families where a member (child or adult) is having psychiatric help, where there is mental sickness in a family or severe degrees of emotional disturbance. Parents are seen regularly by PSWs for psychological help and support over emotional problems and one of their main tasks is to seek and maintain close co-operation with other social welfare agencies.

The Probation officer (PO) is a social worker to the penal system and is primarily a servant of the local administration of the law (the local Courts). Probation came into being as an alternative to a prison sentence or to being sent away to an Approved school or Borstal institution. The Probation officer is the instrument for co-ordinating pre-trial enquiries into home and school background. In addition to collating such information for the Courts, he has regular meetings with children (and adults) whom the Magistrates consider need regular help and counselling support for a defined period of time. Probation officers have other duties which do not concern schools closely—e.g. (a) advisory marriage counselling service in marital disputes where clients can attend on a voluntary basis and do not have to go through the Courts, (b) the after-care of people leaving prison. The probation department has lost some of its responsibilities for young people under sixteen to the new Social Services Department and there may be further government changes arising from the white paper *Children in Trouble* which may influence some of the probation officer's duties (note 3). Such changes, however, are not likely to affect the Juvenile Courts and the Probation officer's relationship with them. If the school is to become more involved than in the past in the prevention of delinquency and of behaviour problems, then close working with both the Child Care officer and the Probation officer becomes likely.

The Child Care officer (CCO) is predominently a local government officer working in the Children's department. (See note 2). A few work for voluntary groups such as Barnardo's and the National Children's Home. These departments were set up by legislation in 1948 by the Children Act whereby each local authority was required to appoint a children's officer to help those children who were unable for any reason to have a home with their parents (either temporarily or permanently). There are several CCOs in each Children's department and other duties include helping to choose foster parents or supervise prospective adoptions of children. Further duties have been added by the 1969 Children and Young Persons Act, which embodied legislation arising from the white paper, *Children in Trouble* (note 3). CCOs also carry out preventive work. They can sometimes prevent the break-up of a family and avoid taking the children into care.

*The Child Guidance Centre or Clinic*

This deals with children of any age, from pre-school to the older adolescent, who show behaviour difficulties or anxiety states either at home or school. A fully staffed centre contains a psychiatrist, educational psychologist (see School Psychological Service below), a psychiatric social worker, a psychotherapist and a secretary. The larger centres have several members of these professions. The psychiatrist is a doctor with special training in child psychiatry and in understanding and treating deviations from the normal affecting the family, and individuals within the family. The psychotherapist has taken a degree in psychology or sociology, is usually a non-medical worker, has had a personal analysis and specialised training in psychotherapy (e.g. at Anna Freud's Child Therapy clinic at Hampstead, London). Children or young people who are selected for treatment are seen regularly on a one-to-one basis to assist in the personal development of those who have been showing impaired relationships with others, while at the same time the family are helped by the PSW. A feature of child guidance work is the conference method and this is discussed later.

*The School Psychological Service (SPS)*

This is staffed by educational psychologists, remedial teachers and occasionally by social workers (in Portsmouth SPS a PSW supervises a group of five social workers who work closely together). The psychologists have an honours degree in psychology supplemented by professional experience of school life and by post-graduate clinical training at a recognised training centre. They work partly in Child Guidance clinics (although to a growing extent independently of them) and partly as advisers on psychological matters to Chief Education officers, to teachers and to parents. This clinical and advisory work aims to make a contribution to the healthy educational and emotional development of all children through the application of psychological knowledge to education generally. To detect and prevent difficulties in normal as well as handicapped children indicates that psychologists have a part to play in the educational process both in and out of school and close connections with the school counsellor are essential. The counsellor's functions are complementary to the psycholgist's functions and there need be no source of conflict here. The former is part of the school staff (and can prove a useful screen for problems for the school psychologist) while the latter serves several schools in an area.

## SUMMARY

The general picture of counselling services in British schools shows a very varied pattern. Most practising school counsellors do some personal counselling and some stress this aspect both as fulfilling the greatest need as well as offering the most help to the staff. The vocational counselling side must not be neglected and close links with the Youth Employment Service, the careers teacher, school social worker and others, to form a Careers Guidance team, is essential.

Effective communication between staff and counsellor needs to be nurtured and the required basis of mutual respect and trust can often be achieved by group meetings *(a)* to discuss problem children and (*b*) general policy problems related to guidance and counselling throughout the school. Case-conference method is a useful device to use, but effective communication will not take place without an awareness of the hidden forces which can disrupt group functioning.

Communication problems exist between school and outside professions and agencies. Continual efforts on the part of the counsellor (and staff) will be necessary to reach out into the community to create and maintain links with certain key people and professions so that each may be able to know when to call for the help of others. Face-to-face contact and knowledge of the other's role are essential for effective communication.

## NOTES

1. E. Irvine ('School-Based Social Work', *New Society* 10 March 1966) advocates a possible extension of the voluntary social worker into schools 'establishing teams composed of about a dozen voluntary

workers attached to a comprehensive or secondary modern school and its tributary primary schools and supervised by a trained organiser, who would herself work with the more difficult families'.

2. It is likely that in the next few years local government will be re-organised in keeping with the Maud Commission proposals, 1969. The white paper on local government re-organisation published in February 1971 constitutes a major reform in local government. Under it Children's Departments have been absorbed in the Social Services Departments which were created by the Local Authority Social Services Act, 1970.

3. The Children and Young Person Act 1969, is intended to bring about major changes in the role of juvenile courts, of the Police, of social workers (especially those in children's departments and the probation service) and of some teachers. The aim of this legislation is to keep children out of juvenile courts whenever possible. When children have to go to juvenile courts the range and quality of provision is likely to be more extensive than at present, more flexibly organised and better adapted to the individual's needs. The Act is intended to put more of the responsibility for helping children and young people in trouble on to social workers, and to take away that responsibility from the courts. The Act came into operation in three stages, the third and last on 1 October 1970. It will be some time before the Act can become fully effective. Instead of the present pattern of local authority remand homes, children's homes, approved schools and reception centres, the Act will provide a single system of community homes.

## FURTHER READING

Some of the most important problems relating to the work of the counsellor in British schools are discussed by Lytton and Craft (66), J. M. Raynor (23), and the symposium on counselling published in *Educ. Res.*, 9, 1967.

A. W. Rowe (83) gives an account of counselling practice in the David Lister Comprehensive School in Hull, and staff and counsellor relationships are explored in some detail in Stewart & Warnath (95, chapter 13).

For some of the early work on vocational counselling probably the best beginning can be made with A. Rodger (6, Chapter 11). Supplemented by Daws (25), Carter (17) and Veness (112). For a list of publications useful in careers and vocational guidance see Appendix A.

For a general survey of social services probably the best up-to-date survey is Phyllis Willmott (127), or Anthony Forder (39).

An excellent summary of current voluntary and statutory social organisations is contained in Pedley (71, pp.100-116). A. Leissner (62) gives detailed descriptions of the kind of family problem dealt with by Children's Officers and CCOs, etc.

Child Guidance can be explored further in MacLean (67) and Khan (59) and the School Psychological Service in a pamphlet of that name (13), and Wall (120).

# 3 Psychological Theory and the Counsellor

## PSYCHOLOGICAL THEORY AND THE COUNSELLOR

It may be true that 'every psychologist has perforce to create his own psychology and that there is little knowledge sufficiently well founded to merit confident application' (Zangwill, 137). To the counsellor this indicates that there will be little help from either the experimental psychologist or from scientific psychology in dealing with the human problems he encounters. In his everyday work the counsellor is continually faced with people who need psychological help and with problems that need to be understood and that demand containment or action. Faced with the fact that no general laws about human behaviour exist that have universal validity and that current resources often break down when confronted with complex human problems the counsellor, in order to make sense of this situation, must draw on different theoretical approaches. In becoming aware of the difficulties in gaining precise knowledge and of the lack of scientific data to support his work he acquires a humility of approach based on uncertainty rather than on certainty. The limitations of theory force him to select ideas from many sources that appear useful in understanding others as well as in studying himself. He will then realise the broad truth that in so far as the counsellor 'knows' himself so he can begin to 'know' other people.

To attempt to apply the results of scientific enquiry to practical affairs can often be hazardous and equivocal as personality theories abound and their mode of application to people is by no means certain. The word 'theory' itself is an over-worked word with emotive associations, overlaid by the prestige coming from the success of scientific theories in advancing technological change and practice, whereas a science of behaviour is still far from realisation. 'Against the perspective of 2,000 years the speed of our advance in studying human nature seems more cheerful. At a rough guess, 200 more years may bring the study of behaviour up to the level which physics reached in Newton's time'. (Broadbent, 14).

From the work of Freud, Bowlby, Klein and many other psychoanalysts the importance of early experience in determining later personality characteristics is elaborated. According to these approaches the main structure of adult character and personality are laid down in early childhood (below the age of five years). There may be, for example, critical periods during which a young child's separation from the mother between the ages of six months and three years can prove severely damaging. It is easy to exaggerate the importance of these early influences and to neglect the influence of social forces that mould the personality. The kinds of reinforcement of the early learning of babyhood and early childhood, and those which occur in later childhood and adolescence, may be just as influential, if not more so, in determining the lines along which the growing person will develop.

Obviously there are influences in personal and family history that can hinder or facilitate psychological growth. Various forms of breakdown between the parents and their offspring can occur at any age. At one extreme the parents can abandon the infant and failure to provide consistent, reliable, and loving parent figures can prove damaging to the growing child (Bowlby, 11). At the other extreme there may be no outward signs of breakdown between parents and children yet the parents may be crucial in inducing other effects on their children that are not necessarily damaging. The parents can determine not only interests and attitudes but the kind of career or job that may be taken up. For example, Hudson (49) suggests that 'There is an excellent case for believing that the origins of the future scientist's bent for analysis lies within the family. Some features of his relations with his parents must discourage an interest in people, and encourage one in objects'.

Different approaches to personality theory are important for the field worker as he may draw from each what he may need when confronted with individual and group problems. This ECLEC-

TICISM is probably seen at its best in what has come to be known as the Case Conference method. This is a more or less formal meeting between professional staff representing different professional skills with a variety of theoretical backgrounds. The aim is to pool such skills and experience in discussing each child and young person, to achieve a synthesis of data from many sources, both subjective and objective, so that appropriate action can flow from a considered diagnosis. In this way hypotheses emerge and an agreed plan evolves. In this way, too, participating staff can often begin to realise how difficult it is to achieve psychological insight into themselves and others.

### THE ROGERIAN APPROACH

An approach to personality in some ways related to the speculative psychoanalytic viewpoint has been developed by the American, C. R. Rogers (80, 81, 82). It has been given different descriptive labels such as 'non-directive' or 'self theory' or 'client-centred'. The essence of his system is a belief in the person as someone who is able to determine what problems should be discussed and who is able to seek his own solutions for them. The person is capable of self-direction; the counsellor's main role is to avoid direct intervention, or to keep such intervention to a minimum.

The most helpful attribute of the counselling interview is seen to be a warm, positive, permissive, accepting attitude on the part of the counsellor which creates the easy environment necessary for change in attitude towards the self to occur. In such a climate, relatively free from threat and anxiety, a move can be made towards accepting those parts of the self which are distasteful or unpleasant. Rogers (82) observes: 'When a person's view of himself changes, his behaviour changes accordingly and to puzzle over this is the beginning of both theory and science'. He analyses the processes making for understanding, such as a feeling for (or empathy with) the other person in a one-to-one situation and a recognition of the reciprocal relationship achieved as one 'imperfect human being' is brought face to face with another 'imperfect human being'. Effective communication in the counsellor-client relationship appears to depend partly on the belief that the individual is capable of self-direction and able to take his own decisions. The person is looked upon as someone who is ready to respond to any or every stimulus outside the self, which performs a control function by searching, sifting and selecting such stimuli on the basis of past experience, of his sense of values and of social norms.

Rogers defines the self as the 'I' or 'me' part of the mind.

> The self-concept, or self-structure, may be thought of as an organised configuration of perceptions of the self which are admissible to awareness. It is composed of such elements as the perception of one's characteristics and abilities; the percepts and concepts of the self in relation to others and to the environment; the value qualities which are perceived as associated with experiences and objects; and goals and ideals which are perceived as having positive or negative valence. (Rogers, 81).

Such a self is subject to the same laws as any other aspect of nature and offers research hypotheses which can be experimentally tested. (Rogers' ideas have proved fruitful in producing such experimental work.) When the individual's image of himself agrees fairly closely with the image others have of him then a degree of stability in adjustment is arrived at. When, however, there are wide differences between such images then instability is a likely result. A self-image is gradually built up based partly on the INTROJECTION of admired individuals, both inside and outside the family. This self-image can so distort his views of himself and the outside world that he defends himself by psychological processes of DENIAL, PROJECTION and RATIONALISATION (see note 1). Rogers considers that progress in personal adjustment is likely to come about when the historical and emotional basis for such distortions is brought to awareness. In this way a more flexible response to experience without such disabling and distorting personal factors is achieved. The counsellor or therapist is seen as a catalyst who helps forward these processes in a relatively unhurried way. The self-image changes through a process of self-acceptance although no definition is offered of the end product or finished state. The individual is always in process of 'becoming'.

### THE PSYCHO-ANALYTIC APPROACH TO PERSONALITY

It is not the intention here to outline the main details in the psycho-analytic approach to personality. This has been done in many recent publications (see Further Reading p.73). The intention is to highlight a few key features which seem to have relevance to counselling. Psychoanalysis is at once a method of helping people who are in psychological distress and a method of scientific investigation into human motivation. In the former case by means of a personal analysis (which is costly both in time and money) it is a form of individual treatment which aims to alleviate, change or cure symptoms. The efficacy of such treatment is difficult to prove in a strictly scientific sense. Psychoanalysis appears as a body of doctrine or as an attempt to present a unified theory of personality development which many claim is useful in education and in social work. Such a viewpoint can at times induce strong emotion in its adherents and in its opponents, although such extreme attitudes are inappropriate for the practitioner who wishes to cull from this approach all that is best and most useful for his work.

The main ideas on personality development derived from psychoanalysis which appear to be useful to the counsellor are:

1. The first few years of life, when the developing child is learning to relate to the parents and to the family, are critical in determining the direction in which a person will develop. How the parents see the child, and how they deal with him, determines how he will regard other people when he becomes adult. His world of people will be seen as hostile, threatening, indifferent or apathetic, depending on how his parents treated him. Fairly characteristic attitudes of suspicion, aggression, or submission will be induced. How the young child reacted to the family setting and system of relationships can often throw light on puzzling aspects of the grown person. The successive stages in infantile sexuality can have great importance in linking certain personality traits in adults with early childhood reaction—for example oral and anal impulses may persist into later life at an unconscious level. Such a view of the importance of the earliest social environment can bring out significant relationships between

parental upbringing, personality and cultural background.

2. Present behaviour is determined largely by the interplay between conscious and unconscious forces. Unconscious forces are present in everyone in the sense that people are not always able to give a full account of their actions and are often puzzled by them. Subsequent reflection can sometimes reveal the unconscious determinents in our behaviour, and the perceptive reader will be able perhaps to supply many examples from his experience. For example, a dislike of a person may be based on infantile feelings of hatred against an important childhood figure. These primitive feelings may be re-aroused much later in life by an adult who resembles this childhood figure either in physical appearance or in manner or attitude. The re-arousal of these primitive feelings may be unpleasant, and not acceptable to consciousness. They may be suppressed and hidden yet they may quite unwittingly still be a factor determining relationships with certain people.

If these unconscious forces in the personality exert such strong influences on behaviour that relationships with others are greatly affected, then it is claimed that behaviour change cannot occur without finding out what these unconscious forces might be. Many psychological processes such as denial, resistance and rationalisation, might have to be overcome before the unconscious conflicts could be understood (Note 1). Some consider that psychoanalytic doctrine should be taught to all those who are going to work professionally with children and young people. For example, Halmos (46) says:

> It is my belief that at the present time a unified theory of personality development must be pivoted on the psychoanalytic theory for no other theory of human motivation available today can offer us explanatory hypotheses of equal scope, depth and predictive power. Nor is there any other theoretical system as helpful as it, both in the handling of human relations in general and in the techniques of professional work in particular.

Although such a claim is a very sweeping one indeed, yet psychoanalytic ideas have permeated much current thinking and have some relevance to counselling practice.

Halmos' views are related to a value or belief system which includes the following propositions:

1. Man has found a way of relieving human unhappiness by a 'faith' in the success of counselling people. By helping others to achieve insight into themselves and to know how they have developed as persons, so people will be enabled to make a better and more satisfying adjustment to living in a mass society. In such a society, and especially in education, it can happen that young people sometimes feel overwhelmed and degraded by mass impersonal teaching where the techniques of instruction can become more important than the nature of the learner. The large size of groups alone can be felt as overpowering; especially if little or no attempt is made to compensate for size and impersonality by contriving an environment where the individual can feel wanted, secure, important and of significance to others.

2. One of the primary tasks of all those professionals engaged in counselling and psychotherapy is to find ways and means of helping others develop insight into themselves. This task is very much part of the belief system of Western philosophic and religious (Christian) tradition, although links with Eastern forms of thought are also detected. Insight is defined by Halmos as 'the individual's ability to relate the affect of a present experience to that of a past one provided the latter determines the basic quality of the former' (45).

3. Each person is of value in and for themselves and 'love for the other' is the basis on which counsellors approach their clients. Help is offered not on the basis of advice-giving or prescription, nor in outlining the causes or reasons for maladjustment, but those counselled are invited to discover the truth about themselves in a non-directive way. This does not mean that the 'fiction of non-directiveness' can be permanently maintained as some direction based on moral commitment must inevitably take place, however unwittingly. The 'faith of the counsellors' has 'implicitly retained the notion of an unanalysable proclivity and need to love and to be loved'. The re-emergance of behaviouristic and mechanical ideas based on Pavlovian methods has made 'a mutual accommodation with traditional moral images of love impossible' while 'the vitalistic psychological teaching of

psycho-analytically orientated counsellors has . . . underpinned and perpetuated traditional moral confidence in a humanistic and noble conception of human love' (47, p.194).

### THE BEHAVIOURIST APPROACH

The approaches to counselling so far considered are based on the view that changes in behaviour and attitude are possible by concentrating on the subjective and introspective, on feelings and emotion and by paying attention to inner experience. A contrasting view which seems to exclude at first sight nearly all the hypothetical ideas put forward by the psychoanalysts and the self-theory school is based on the premise that only objectively observable behaviour is admissible in science. Since most human behaviour is acquired by learning then it ought to be possible to contrive conditions in which undersirable behaviour can be 'unlearned' and desirable behaviour either learned or re-learned. To modify behaviour, a degree of manipulation is inevitable and new learning conditions are consciously planned based on learning theory and the results of experimental work. From a behaviouristic viewpoint the counselling can be seen as a means of re-arranging environmental conditions based on CONDITIONING techniques. These techniques, rigorously planned in an objective way, deal directly with individual problems and symptoms. Any attempt at understanding, at gaining insight or at empathy is consciously avoided. The approach to the person is made by isolating the problem (and this can be anything from a reading disability to compulsive masturbation) and by designing an experiment which may modify or eliminate such a problem. Attention is concentrated on separate elements of behaviour, and some success has been reported. One variant of these techniques is known as behaviour therapy or behavioural counselling and the utility of this approach is described at length in Eysenck (35), Woody (132) or Rachman (74).

The Skinnerian model is often taken as an example of applied science where an attempt is made to shape behaviour using procedures derived from widely accepted theories and experimental practices rather than from those which appear to be unduly speculative. Skinner's ideas seem to be characterised by a tremendous optimism about their beneficial outcome or end-result and by a strong faith in the value of his reinforcement techniques.

Skinner maintains that the learning of any task must be split up into many small successive steps and that as each step is carried out it must be reinforced. He defines reinforcement objectively as anything which increases the probability of an action being repeated. Reinforcement can take many different forms such as material rewards (for example a sweet) or a reward such as praise by a teacher, or even the awareness that the action carried out is the correct one. Each step must be mastered properly and correctly, and be reinforced appropriately before the learner goes on to the next step. Each step is worked out in such a way as to appear to follow on naturally from the preceding one and becomes in its turn a preparation for the next. The overall aim is to ensure a rapid and immediate success in mastering each step. It is more effective to reinforce correct learning than to criticise adversely the incorrect.

The model offered by Skinner has been used as a basis for educational programming (for example in teaching machines) as well as for providing a theoretical background for dealing with severe behaviour problems in schools. The utility value of Skinner's approach is seen in a study by Wagner (117) where he shows how it is possible to apply Skinnerian ideas in order to eliminate a severe behaviour problem, the compulsive public masturbation of an eleven-year-old girl.

Wagner assumed that certain behaviour changes are required in a certain direction—the girl had to stop compulsive masturbation in front of the class. To stop this behaviour he selected certain reinforcing agents as a form of reward. These proved momentarily inhibiting to the child when introduced. These reinforcing agents were activities she particularly enjoyed such as painting, handing out and collecting papers, helping the teacher, and so on. Whenever masturbation stopped a reward was offered immediately thus ensuring that the desired response pattern was repeated. Unwanted responses went unrewarded and soon vanished because of non-reinforcement. The number of rewards increased as the desired behaviour gradually became more frequent. For example, when one full day had been completed without masturbation a special note was sent to the parents to say how well she had behaved that day. By arrangement with the parents it was agreed that they would reward her successes suitably on receiving these notes from the teacher. The position was eventually reached when the desired response pattern was regularly being shown. The experimenter also manipulated other variables such as the spacing of rewards thus ensuring experimental control of the desired behaviour.

The principles behind Skinner's approach are perhaps fairly easy to grasp although any serious attempt at experimenting with behaviour therapy methods needs to be carried out by someone specially trained in their use. As Broadbent observes (14, p.133), 'The whole virtue of Skinner's attitude is that it draws attention to the concrete realities of behaviour', although obviously one of the dangers can be that alternative explanations and theories may be ignored or neglected. The same result might well have been achieved here by a different method of approach or the result achieved may have been due to the skilful, co-operative and understanding teacher who regularly received support from someone outside the school, thus reducing any anxiety that may have been present. (Note 2).

## THE INFLUENCE OF TRAIT AND FACTOR THEORIES

That people differ in all sorts of ways one from another is a commonplace observation. The counsellor, however, must be alert to the extremely wide variations in ability, temperament, interests, attitudes, beliefs and values because detailed knowledge of these variations forms the basis of all work with human beings. The trait and factor approach is a way of applying tests or objective measurements to people so that a measure of the extent of this wide variation becomes possible.

The responses to questionnaires and other objective personality tests can be classified by a mathematical technique known as FACTOR ANALYSIS. This is an attempt to classify large numbers of people and to identify the traits or dimensions controlling behaviour by mathematical comparisons of the results of tests applied to these individuals. These traits or dimensions can be said to vary along a continuum showing that most people will possess some of the trait or dimension. At the ends of the continuum there are but a few who possess the trait in its extreme form. Vernon (115) referring to the analysis of ability tests, describes these dimensions as 'a kind of blurred average'. In this country perhaps the foremost representative of this point of view in personality research is Professor H. J. Eysenck. He offers a hierarchical description of personality organisation where specific habits form the base above which are grouped traits. These in turn are grouped into a few major categories or dimensions. These dimensions or types are claimed to be the results emerging from a factor analysis of a large number of test results. In this way PSYCHOTICS can be distinguished from NEUROTICS and both from normals. He claims that three main dimensions or types can be recognised: 1. the dimension neuroticism—NORMALITY (Eysenck 37); 2. INTROVERSION—EXTRAVERSION (ibid p.59); and 3. PSYCHOTICISM— normality. In like fashion social attitudes can be reduced to the dimensions radicalism—conservatism and to tough-mindedness—tender-mindedness.

While there is no agreement amongst experts as to the value of this approach either in understanding people or in counselling, yet the material (questionnaires, inventories and so on) produced as a result of this work can sometimes be useful to the counsellor to help him with his contacts with groups. For example, discussions can be sparked off by the filling in of questionnaires, or inventories can often help in the selection of individuals for counselling.

However, one of the main weaknesses of the trait and factor approach lies partly in the relative instability of the test scores and their lack of consistency, and partly in the uncertain psychological meaning of the factors or traits.

## PERSONALITY GROWTH IN ADOLESCENCE

If, for convenience, we divide the period from birth to the fully grown person into three periods—childhood, adolescence and adulthood—then it is important to remember that there is no sharp dividing line between them. The physical changes of adolescence occur somewhere between ages ten to fourteen years for girls and between eleven to sixteen years for boys. There are wide individual differences in the length of adolescence and these ages should only be taken as very approximate guides.

It is important for the counsellor to distinguish between two aspects of adolescence. On the one hand there are the physical changes connected with puberty, and on the other hand, psycho-social phenomena—the growing adolescent is affected in countless ways by his family and by the larger society outside the family. The counsellor needs to know how physical changes at puberty can affect the adolescent and also how the adolescent sees himself in relation to others, his friends, relations and contemporaries.

While the main lines of character may have been laid down in the early years, and the foundations for the rapid changes in adolescence have been laid in the period covering the primary school (up to the age of eleven) yet there are several characteristics of adolescent development which create a peculiar challenge for a counsellor. The counselling of the age group ten to sixteen is rewarding for the opportunity it offers for giving help at a time when it is most acutely needed.

*Physical Changes*

Adolescence is a time of rapid physical change and growth, forming an idiosyncratic pattern for each individual. The adolescent spurt is a universal and constant phenomenon varying in length and intensity from one child to another and, during this period, there is a rapid alteration in the shape of the body with chemical and glandular changes taking place. Whether an individual is an early or late maturer, the psychological repercussions of these physical changes may be considerable. Girls appear to be physically and emotionally more advanced at all ages than boys. Early-maturing boys appear likely to excel in school athletics and 'perhaps get more than their share of appointments to social distinction also'. (Tanner 103).

Rapid alterations in girth and height obviously influence the image built up of the body and lead to changes in co-ordination of limbs and motor patterns. 'The adolescent in general appears to be pre-occupied with physical appearance and status; the girl whose breasts are beginning to develop may refuse to stand erect, but slouches instead when asked to recite in front of the class'. (103). The body changes related to physical growth are closely linked with the beginnings of a rather sudden and dramatic sexual functioning. The adolescent concentrates intensely on his body, and is interested in how it works, and in the nature of the physical changes through which he is going. Both sexes are often ready at this stage for formal lessons in elementary human anatomy and physiology and may be further interested in related topics from the details of personal hygiene to a discussion of the religious and cultural taboos on the expression of the sex drive. The late developer may be puzzled about his apparent failure to grow at the rate of his contemporaries and may want to know more about the physical details of growth. Those who mature early have adjustment problems also. They have to wait longer than the average young person before career aspirations can be realised. Correspondingly a longer period of frustration of the sex drive is likely. The position is summarised aptly by Tanner (104, p.49):

> Adolescence, with the arousal of the sex drive, is a time of intense concentration on the body. This may take any form from the crude simple-minded competitive comparisons of sexual apparatus and functions in the happy-go-lucky extraverts of residential school, or boys club hut, to the solitary guilt-laden brooding of the sensitive, shy boy, afraid to confide his half-realised problems to anyone except perhaps to an unusually perspicacious family doctor or an experienced and sympathetic youth leader. Much of the anxiety about sex is, of course, at an unconscious level and proceeds from sources that are considerably more complex and deep-rooted than these. Yet even here, the events—or lack of events—of adolescence may act as a trigger to reverberate fears accumulated deep in the mind during the early years of life . . . afraid that one's skills, one's possessions in the purely non-material sense, will be taken away from one or denigrated.

*Understanding Sexual Development*

During the years ten to fifteen endocrine development prepares the younger generation for eventual mating and reproduction. The home and parents are of great importance in influencing the smooth development of the sex drive, for from parents the adolescent develops his idea of the sex role in the family. Identification with admired figures, both inside and outside the family may also take place. The nature of this identification influences his attitude towards his own sexuality, and he relates it to family attitudes and towards religious and cultural taboos. In this process teachers' and the school community's influence is probably only marginal when sex education is offered in a formal way, and as another teaching subject. When, however, sex is treated not just as an isolated problem on its own but as part of the wider topic of personal relationships generally then a different view of sex education becomes possible. By widespread use of small, informal groups meeting regularly, led by a teacher or other professional skilled in handling group counselling, a more effective approach to sex teaching may be achieved. The age at which sex education should be given in schools is in dispute. Some maintain that it should begin not later than the nine- to ten-year age group (see for example Chanter, 20). There is general agreement, however, that sex education should begin much earlier than it does at present.

Many consider that sex education has to be offered in schools as there are many young people who are not helped adequately by parents. Schofield (84) reported that two-thirds of the boys and a quarter of the girls in his own sample had heard nothing about sex from their parents. He mentions that the teacher was the second most important source of sex knowledge for boys and the third most important for girls. There was not only an easily demonstrated need in his sample for sex education in schools but teenagers are anxious to be informed about sex 'provided it is given with an assurance that it is backed by knowledge and with a proper understanding of their particular problems' (84, p.250). For some, he maintains, it will mean individual counselling.

The fallacy behind much present day sex education is that the apparent need seems to be for more and better information. But the information will often be construed differently by different people and the central problem of studying how to improve the quality of personal relationships can easily be by-passed.

It is particularly important in schools that a high degree of skill is brought to bear in sex education otherwise it is probably best not attempted. A number of conditions need to be satisfied for success. As suggested previously sex education should be treated as a part of the more general problem of personal relationships. The person to offer the sex education must be specially selected as having the right personal qualities and, if possible, as having special training for this work. Sometimes this can be someone from outside the school, such as a marriage guidance counsellor, a member of the school medical service, a representative of the Family Planning Association, a local doctor, or other appropriate professional. The co-operation of all parents needs to be assured by preliminary discussions and by close involvement in the planning of suitable programmes. It is important that good relationships with the children are established. Some attempt at follow-up—by small discussion groups, for example—in the older age groups, after the initial programme, can prove rewarding. Such a repeat programme in a different setting offers an opportunity for using different material, perhaps by showing suitable films (Note 3) for reinforcing previous information and for trying out more appropriate discussion methods. The older and more sensitive adolescent can write down questions anonymously so preventing embarrassment, and ensuring that urgent and meaningful questions are asked and answered.

*Psychological Changes*

To attempt generalisations on adolescence is to invite the charge either of superficiality, of presenting a false picture or of going beyond the evidence. The picture drawn may not apply to the individual case and may require considerable modification as fads, fashions, opinions and prejudices alter, and the facts from research accumulate. It is not possible to say with any precision in what way present-day attitudes of adults towards adolescents, or of adolescents towards society, are different from those of other ages or cultural patterns. Today's adolescent strives for an independence from parents that cannot always be satisfied. Freedom from parent control is desired but society and family cannot always allow it. His skills and knowledge are not developed enough for them to satisfy the level demanded by the adult and hence he cannot be treated or accepted as an equal. More young people stay on at school beyond age fifteen and this enlarges the number who delay progress towards independence and who strive to reach adult status but are unable to do so because of age, level of skills or experience. The attendant ambiguity and uncertainty can be reflected in the adult attitude varying from indifference and withdrawal to hostile and aggressive reactions often with unfortunate side effects. Tolerance, friendly feelings, understanding, patience and forbearance appear difficult virtues to practise. Doing things with adolescents, rather than to, for, or against them, seems a difficult rule to follow.

The role of anxiety in the adolescent is summarised by Wall (119, p.8) who suggests that the basic psychological problem is one of anxiety.

The prolongation of dependence well into the second half of the second decade of life, the widening range of differences in status which occurs from age fifteen onwards, the uncertainties in adults about what to do and what to expect, and the increasing tendency to project on to the whole teenage group, stereotypes applicable only at the margins, conspire to produce uncertainty as to the role expected from adolescents by society. The role of the school boy or girl is fairly clear; the roles of the adult as bread winner, citizen, husband or wife and son also seem clear. Attitudes to the boy and girl who stay on at school after fifteen, or who enter work and part-time education and training, are ambiguous and ambivalent. In certain institutionalised ways, entry to adulthood is delayed . . . schools and families may be even more ambivalent, expecting responsible behaviour without according the right to make responsible decisions for oneself, jealously or fearfully striving to suppress or ignore rising sexuality whilst at the same time leaving pubertal boys and girls exposed to the titillation and solicitation of advertising and the mass media, urging them to form personal viewpoints and standards of values . . . [and] . . . refusing, or at best failing, to state and defend their own points of view and beliefs . . . the adolescent is teetering on the brink without much in the way of guidance or reassurance on which to found his security.

Most young people need help from secure and easily available adults to support them through these growth problems although the amount of disabling stress arising from these conflicts may be small. There are many positive features of adolescence which give grounds for optimism. It is a time when goals are discussed and defined and there is a steady working towards them without too much stress for the majority. It is a time of intellectual excitement, the free exchange of ideas and a striving towards academic excellence, although difficulties may occur in the acceptance of imposed skills and knowledge which appear to have only the most tenuous relationship with future goals. The adolescent searches continually for a meaning in life, for a philosophy to live by and for the means to develop a scale of values. Questions such as Who am I? What am I going to become? How am I compared with my contemporaries? How am I going to earn my living?—these are some of the preoccupations of the adolescent. Different kinds of outlet are needed for idealism and the sense of challenge in overcoming natural forces seems essential for some. (Schemes on the lines of the 'Outward Bound' organisation for example, or foreign adventure travel as perhaps a downward extension of the Voluntary Service Overseas.) As the transition takes place from adolescence to adulthood, so the boundaries between phantasy and reality become sharper and clearer although never, perhaps, completely disappearing. As D. W. Winnicott says (130), 'The cure for adolescence belongs to the passage of time and to the gradual maturation processes; these together do in the end result in the emergence of the adult person'. The experience of living, for most people, is itself therapeutic.

## SUMMARY

The counsellor needs a background knowledge of some approaches to personality theories. These are of such bewildering forms and variety that only those need be considered which will aid the counsellor in his approach to people.

The approaches to personality which appear to have the greatest utility value for the counsellor are those on the one hand representing the subjective and the introspective—and based largely on the Rogerian model, the non-directive—and on the other hand those stressing the objective and based mostly on conditioning techniques allied to a Skinnerian model.

These two contrasting approaches are not necessarily mutually exclusive although it is perhaps unlikely that they will both be equally successful in the hands of one counsellor.

The school and the counsellor are involved in helping the new generation through their physical and psychological growth problems. This includes offering sexual information, linked with a more general knowledge of how the body works covering perhaps aspects of physiology and anatomy within a context of an intensive study of the factors that make for good communication between people.

## NOTES

1. For a discussion of some of these 'ego defence mechanisms' see Lovell (64, chapter 4) or C. Rycroft, *A Critical Dictionary of Psycho-Analysis* (Nelson 1968).

2. There are many factors leading to successful results. The faith and confidence in a particular outcome can induce greater efforts amongst participants. The desired behaviour may be produced by cues, hints and suggestions given unwittingly or sub-consciously. Again, observations may be biased by rigidly pre-conceived ideas—expectations and prophecies become self-fulfilling and you find what you expect to find. Factors other than the ones put forward as influencing results are mentioned in Southgate's (93) discussion on the introduction of a new alphabet (ITA) for the teaching of reading in schools. The success claimed for the experimental classes could be accounted for by factors other than the introduction of such an alphabet (e.g. the teachers' faith in the new method, an inability to control all the variables satisfactorily, the change of attitude when a reading drive is started in a school, increased enthusiasm for a new method and so on). Higher reading standards can flow from a reading drive irrespective of what methods or schemes are used in the teaching of reading.

3. There are many films on sex education. Some of them which have proved useful to counsellors are: 'From Boy to Man'; 'To Janet a Son'; 'Girl to Woman'; 'Woman of Tomorrow'; 'Sex is Everywhere'. Many teachers and counsellors have also used with success television programmes such as the Grampian Television sex education programmes.

## FURTHER READING

Perhaps one of the best introductory guides to human growth and development is written by a psychiatrist, Khan (58). The chapters on infancy, childhood and adolescence, are a good introduction to developmental stages from a psychiatric point of view. As a counter-balance to this medical viewpoint see Lovell (chapter 5 of 64 or chapter 4 of 63).

The literature on psychoanalysis is vast. The easiest available, with serviceable bibliographies, are Brown (15) and Storr (96). Peter Blos *On Adolescence* (The Free Press of Glencoe, 1962) is an excellent account of psycho-analytic views of children.

Halmos' views are mostly contained in his most recent book (47).

Rogers' summary (82) of his personality theory is a concentrate of his various viewpoints developed earlier (80, 81), all of which should be read by those who wish to become deeply acquainted with the non-directive viewpoint.

Wagner's article (117) must be consulted for the details of his application of Skinnerian method. The best original source for Skinner's ideas is probably (90) while a useful supplement is either chapter 5 of O'Connor (68) or chapter 4 of Borger and Seaborne (9). The student interested in an advanced form of high level thinking illustrating the give and take of scientific argument could not improve on Broadbent where he criticises Skinner's viewpoint (14, pp.132-137). This is difficult reading, however.

Eysenck (37, chapter 4), Rachman (74) and Eysenck (35) introduce behaviour therapy concepts. Of more relevance to the educational counsellor is Woody (132 and 133) and the same author attempts a rapprochement between behaviour therapy and psychotherapy. (*B.J.Med.Psych.* Vol. 41, Pt. 3, 1968).

Tanner (103 and 104) should be read for throwing light on the relationship between physical facts and education.

Wall (119) gives useful bibliographies in his latest book together with a critique of the literature relating to the results of research on adolescence.

The books on sex education most relevant to counselling are Tame (102) and Chanter (20) plus Dawkins, *A Textbook of Sex Education* (Blackwell, Oxford, 1967) and Beck, *Human Growth* (Gollancz, 1961).

# 4 Aspects of appraisal in Schools

## ASPECTS OF APPRAISAL IN SCHOOLS

There are three routes by which information can be gleaned when making assessments on children or adults: by observation, by introspection or self-report, and by objective records of performance. Each of these areas is essential in order to arrive at a balanced picture and to reduce the risk of errors. Observation by itself is plainly insufficient because personal opinion, preconceived ideas, and prejudice may distort what is seen; also there is great variability between people in observational skills. Yet the virtues of just watching others closely must not be disregarded as significant observations may be offered which are missed or ignored by other approaches. Teachers are here in an advantageous position for making sustained observations which are unique because they are in day-to-day contact with large numbers of children and young people over long periods of time.

There is a sense in which no test can tell you anything that you cannot get equally well from observation; but the time available for observing may be limited or personal factors may intervene, such as fatigue towards the end of term, or flagging vigilance if observations are too prolonged. The acute observer can often distinguish without tests the able from the less able, the unstable personality from those of even temperament, the dull intellect from the severely sub-normal. Specific educational difficulties can often be spotted easily enough without objective tests (e.g. in reading or spelling) and the withdrawn, shy, sensitive child distinguished from the sociable, the popular and the extraverted.

The limitations of introspection are equally obvious when it is realised that what a person says about himself cannot always be relied on with complete confidence. Unrealistic ambitions or ideas, unwitting distortions or selection of the evidence in order to put oneself in the most favourable light, are met with constantly. However, introspection is sometimes the only way of finding out how the other person sees his world and is thus of importance in the counselling interview.

It is essential then to balance observation and self-report by using objective methods. These can be of many kinds varying from STANDARDISED TESTS to a tape-recording of an interview. A test is an attempt to sample behaviour objectively by means of a rating or score derived from procedures described in the test manual and based on adequate standardisation data. The reader can get some impression of the bewildering array of such tests in current use by consulting current test catalogues (Note 1). Some general training in test administration and interpretation on those tests which can be used by teachers is desirable, but certain tests can only be used when very specialised training has been given. A knowledge of test construction, methods of standardisation and of their limitations is essential (Note 2). Inadequate training or a failure to master the principles of testing (often called PSYCHOMETRICS) could perhaps mean harm or injustice to the person tested either through errors in administration or in interpretation. A high level of skill is needed in planning a testing programme and in interpreting the scores, and some schools have a teacher or counsellor concentrating on this alone. It is inappropriate in a book of this nature to give a systematic and comprehensive description of tests that might be useful to the counsellor. Many of the practical details of testing are best dealt with by training courses: the kinds of test the counsellor may or may not use for professional reasons; the usefulness or otherwise of tests to the counsellor; how to interpret test information coming from outside agencies; the uses and limitations of different kinds of test.

All objective tests can be either of the group or the individual. Group tests, as their name implies, can be given to large numbers of children and people at once. Occasionally group tests can be given individually (e.g. the Raven's progressive matrices test). One important point to remember with the interpretation of group test scores is that while the overall pattern of scores can give a fairly accurate account of group characteristics, yet any individual score within this overall pattern may be totally unreliable. Often there is no way of assessing this accurately in any individual case if the score is a low one and without an individual investigation. When it is a high one the score can be regarded as more likely to be nearer the true score. However, repeated group measurements over a period of time, or other supporting evidence such as an individual test, or observations of the classroom teacher, are necessary if any important decisions are to be taken. Ideally, continuous testing over the years should be the rule and the results recorded systematically. Group tests are not appropriate for certain children or students, for example, for those with disturbed personalities, or for those with a particular handicap such as a reading disability. Most group verbal intelligence and English tests need a reading age of at least nine years, as measured by a standardised graded word reading test, before the scores can begin to have meaning.

Individual tests are standardised by being given to each individual separately and can be administered only by a qualified psychologist (either clinical or educational) since specialised training is necessary before they can be used (see Note 3). Whenever there is any doubt about the intellectual level of a child or young person, then the services of a trained psychologist should be called in to help in appraisal.

Tests can be classified according to the purpose for which they are intended. *Attainments* tests show how an individual might compare with others in an area of the curriculum such as English, mechanical arithmetic, spelling or reading. Here a particular skill is taught and an assessment made of the level of skill reached in comparison with others. Tests of *general intellectual ability* (or *intelligence*) throw some light on an individual's ability to reason and capacity to learn. Tests here can be divided roughly into two types; those involving abstract reasoning and ability to solve problems by words, numbers or symbols, and on the other hand those involving non-verbal abilities (sometimes called performance tests). Tests of *special aptitudes* can offer a measure of such special abilities as musical or mechanical ability. Tests of *interests* can sometimes be used to get a measure of an individual's liking for certain ways of thinking or particular activities. They can sometimes throw light on the direction of vocational thinking. Tests of *personality* are used frequently in research to attempt to measure a complex of temperamental and character qualities which make the individual unique. They can be used to describe a group on a series of personality dimensions or to survey a large number for screening for particular problems. The majority of personality tests are too technical or too highly specialised for counsellors to use, and are in most cases not relevant to his work. *Diagnostic or clinical* tests are not perhaps strictly tests in the manner defined here as they do not yield a score and are used qualitatively, in a clinic or hospital setting. The only exceptions are certain educational tests such as the Schonell diagnostic arithmetic tests where a formal and systematic attempt is made to find out the arithmetical processes which are not known by the subject, or where difficulty is encountered. (Note 4).

Group tests are probably of the greatest help in assessment when used as a form of continuous educational guidance covering most of school life. Such testing is not worthwhile below the age of eight unless it is done for a specific project or by means of individual tests. When important vocational decisions have to be taken later in school life then they are best based on extended observations covering a number of years rather than on a single interview towards the end of school life. In planning such continuous educational assessment the test user needs some technical knowledge of how tests are constructed and standardised, how to express test scores so that they can be compared one with another and the meaning of test score patterns for individuals. Every test user must have certain basic information about a test before it can be used with any degree of confidence and this should always be available in the manual accompanying the test. This will include the age range covered by the test, the purpose of the test, the possible applications it might have, directions for administering and scoring, specific merits of the tests, tables of NORMS together with some indication perhaps of how the scores might be used in the manner intended, the kind and nature of the population used in standardisation, and an estimate of the errors of measurement. Great caution is needed in choosing tests, and in selecting them for a particular purpose since even with the most careful safeguards complete adequacy in standardisation is probably rarely achieved and many tests are on the market which are out of date or apply to a different population from the one available. (See the BPS publication, 13, for further information).

## SOME KEY CONCEPTS IN TESTING

Some estimate of the dependability of test scores needs to be made and the technical term 'reliability' is used to indicate the extent of this dependability. For example, if the same test were repeated after a defined interval of time, the reliability is a measure of the stability of scores—a measure of the degree to which the individuals making up the standardisation sample are likely to achieve the same score on repetition. This reliability can be estimated in a number of ways, but a useful rule for test users is that whenever possible only tests with a reliability of 0.9 or greater should be used. An alternative measure of reliability is given in every good test by the standard error of measurement (SEm), a statistic which gives an estimate of the likelihood that the obtained test score is a measure of the true score. It is an estimate of the limits beyond which any future scores are unlikely to go.

Approximately two-thirds of all scores obtained for a test will be within $\pm 1$ SEm of their 'true' score: and approximately 95 per cent within $\pm 2$ SEm. For example, if a test has a standard error of measurement of 2.5 points (on a scale of standardised scores), then approximately 95 per cent of the observed scores will lie within $\pm 5$ points of their 'true' score. Another way of saying the same thing is that, with this test, the 'true' scores of 19 out of 20 children taking it will lie within $\pm 5$ points of their obtained scores. In only one case in 20 is the 'true' score likely to be outside these limits. (Pidgeon 72).

Every test manual should state the degree to which the quality claimed to be measured is in fact measured. This is the technical term called 'validity' and is expressed by means of a validity coefficient. This is a measure of the degree of association between the behaviour measured by the test and a criterion agreed as a trustworthy measure of the quality in question and arising from previous investigations. It takes the form of a correlation coefficient (as in reliability above) but never reaches the level of a reliability coefficient, e.g. a validity coefficient more than 0.75 or 0.80 would be considered to be exceptionally high.

There are many ways of expressing test scores, some of which are considerably more technical than others and are not of direct relevance to the counsellor. It has become accepted practice in schools testing to express scores as standardised scores, which are based on a mean of 100 and a standard deviation of 15 (see Pidgeon and Yates, 73, for an explanation of these terms). With individual ability tests such as the Wechsler Adult Intelligence Scale (WAIS) (125) or the Wechsler Intelligence Scale for Children (WISC) (124), it is still common practice to quote scores in terms of IQ rather than of standardised scores.

The interpretation of test scores requires then a great deal of practice, training and knowledge. A series of measurements over a number of years can sometimes reveal interesting problems. As an example of such a problem taken from my notebooks, the following pattern of scores on group tests was obtained by a boy aged eight years five months when first tested the last test being given at age twelve years three months:

*Richard's Pattern of Test Scores*

| *Age* | *Intelligence Quotient (IQ)* | *English Quotient (EQ)* | *Arithmetic Quotient (AQ)* |
|---|---|---|---|
| 8 years 5 months | 104 | 108 | 132 |
| 9 years 5 months | 106 | 125 | 128 |
| 10 years 6 months | 129 | 105 | 122 |
| 12 years 3 months | 136 | 131 | 128 |

The IQ (or Verbal Reasoning) tests used here and elsewhere were NFER Primary Verbal 1; NFER Primary Verbal 2; NFER closed test; Moray House Intelligence Test No. 23. All the other tests were of this quality and were mostly NFER tests.

The results of the first testing suggested either that he was a boy of good average general ability and average English ability (with perhaps a special aptitude for number) or that he was possibly a boy of above average ability under-functioning on the verbal side, and possibly held back by low reading ability. He was tested individually on a reading test on which he scored at an average level for his age (Vernon (113), reading age 8.8 years); this was corrected since the original test was based on Scottish norms which are approximately half a year in advance of the English norm at this age. There were clues from his behaviour that he might possibly be an able boy. It so happened that his teacher was interested in the application to the whole class of the SRA Programmed Reading Material (Form 11b) (Note 5). Partly as a result of this concentration on his reading skills Richard was one of the pupils who made rapid progress in reading and within nine months his reading age had gone up to nearly twelve years. Such a rapid advance in reading skill was not completely reflected in his test score on the intelligence test. From about aged ten onwards Richard's social and emotional development showed changes towards more self-confidence, increased participation in classroom activities and a widening circle of friends. At age eight years he had been rather shy and with little disposition to mix with others apart from one close friend. None of this behaviour was considered by his teacher to be in any way abnormal. When Richard was retested in his Secondary School his scores placed him in the top two per cent for ability and attainment for his age and this was confirmed by his placement in his form. Every teacher is aware of children's variablity in performance and this can occur at any age. In Richard's case his final status intellectually and educationally proved very high indeed when he was seen for individual testing, scoring a verbal IQ on the WISC (125) of 145 (at age thirteen-and-a-half years) and a reading age on the Vernon of over seventeen years.

Apart from errors arising from the tests themselves, errors can arise because of the many influences external to the test which can interfere with the results. Most children will fail to give of their best unless they wish to and this is unlikely to happen unless they have been suitably prepared. Even so, no matter how well the testing programme is conceived or how well the tester tries to make effective contact with his groups, it will be impossible to control all the complexities of attitude and motivation or to allow for some personal reactions and inadequacies (these are perhaps easier to control in individual testing but never completely so). Psychometric testing, too, has other disadvantages, in that test scores can be treated as labels leading to rigidity of thinking and to the neglect of the subtleties of interpretation. Scores on tests are only the very beginning of the study of children and young people and provide only a small part, even if an important one, of the total assessment, when evidence is drawn from many different sources. There are, too, large geographical and regional variations in mean test scores.

Standardised tests, however, have advantages apart from the objectivity mentioned previously. They are a speedy way of getting some basic information about groups and about some individuals within the group. They can be useful for diagnostic purposes, e.g. for contributing towards a plan for remedial work. The results can be used, too, as a basis for individual interviews or for counselling. Great caution, however, as well as skill, is needed before psychometric information is given to individuals; it must be given in the right form without causing upset or harm and with no possibility of misrepresentation or misinterpretation. Frequent staff changes or other staffing difficulties sometimes prevent adequate assessments of classroom groups and an objective testing programme might be helpful in these circumstances. New and recently trained staff can often improve the quality of their observations by usung objective measures as a guide and by helping to establish standards.

*The counsellor's view of achievement*

Whatever views are held about examinations (whether they should be based externally on the GCE pattern, for example, or whether they should be based as well on continuous assessment of the individual by teachers or by objective-type tests) there is no doubt whatever that academic success and progress, assuming an optimum school environment for facilitating learning, depends on three factors. These are:

(*a*) intelligence,

(*b*) level of reading skill, and

(*c*) the drive to achieve.

Each of these areas can offer difficulties for the teacher and for the counsellor.

It is notoriously difficult to get agreement amongst experts as to what is meant by intelligence or how to define or measure it. Many doubts have been expressed on the value of intelligence tests and even their name has been changed to verbal reasoning tests or tests of general mental ability. At least three meanings of the term have lately been distinguished. Firstly, there is Intelligence A, which represents innate ability and suggests inferences about genetic differences between individuals. It is rarely possible for Intelligence A to be measured or even observed with complete accuracy. Intelligence B which results from the interaction of the genetic potential and the cultural environment and accords closely with the observable all-round ability in daily life at work or at school and can be described as quickness in thinking or sound practical judgment. Thirdly, there are the scores on conventional intelligence tests for which Vernon has suggested the name 'Intelligence C.' Vernon (116) has suggested adding a further meaning to intelligence, which he calls 'constitutional intelligence or physiological potentiality', the development of which is related to 'physiological conditions before birth, on adequate proteins and vitamins in the diet particularly from about —3 to +6 months. . . . All these undoubtedly affect the building up of healthy brain tissue and its capacity for further development'. For Western society there is no doubt that intelligence tests have considerable predictive value vocationally and educationally. For example, Eysenck (35) writes:

The results of very large numbers of carefully planned investigations support the conclusion that IQ tests, properly constructed, administered and evaluated show considerable agreement with the success of the child at school, or the adolescent at the University.

The importance of repeated measurements on IQ tests can be seen in the following:

*Tom's Pattern of Test Scores*

| *Age* | *VR* | *EQ* | *AQ* |
|---|---|---|---|
| 8 years 7 months | 102 | 104 | 108 |
| 9 years 7 months | 101 | 103 | — |
| 10 years 8 months | 110 | 107 | 109 |
| 12 years 5 months | 144 | 108 | 108 |

It was only by repeated testing that the one isolated score of 144 was noticed as an indication of something unusual. This led to testing with an individual intelligence test (Terman-Merrill Binet Form L/M, 1960 revision) where his IQ came out at 155 and his reading age on the Vernon was 17.7 years. Such high ability had not been detected by his teachers partly because he was a quiet, retiring, and rather passive, person with little urge to join in class activities or to show his ability by answering questions in class. His particular class, too, had had a succession of teachers, some of whom had to leave through illness and other distressing circumstances. None of his teachers had taught him for longer than about a term and a half.

*The development of reading skill*

The ability to read widely and well at any age is plainly important for academic success. While the most skilled readers tend to be the more intelligent people the correspondence is far from being perfect. Reading skill, in children especially, is a very complex ability. Concentrated diagnostic resources, matched by appropriate remedial methods, need to be brought to bear at the right time in order to prevent the appearance of a disabling reading handicap. The effects of reading failure, or of underfunctioning at reading, can be seen at any age and stage in schools. There is the eight year old who begins to be sensitive about not being able to translate symbols which everyone else seems to master. There is the intelligent adolescent whose level of reading skill is well below what it could be. Children in primary schools between the ages of seven and nine who have a suspected reading disability should always be assessed as early as possible by an educational psychologist. To make remedial measures most effective such children should be identified by the age of eight. There are many causes for a reading disability. When low intelligence can be ruled out, the main causes can often be sought in a breakdown in the parent-child relationships at home and/or in the failure of the child to be given appropriate help at the right time within the school. (Note 6).

Reading ability seems to develop in three stages, each stage merging imperceptibly into the other. The first stage represents the acquisition of a 'sight' vocabulary of about 400-500 words (this is equivalent to a reading age between six and seven years on a conventional graded word reading test). Such a 'sight' vocabulary can be acquired in many ways depending partly on the child's preferences for particular modes of learning. A mixture of methods on the part of the teacher is usually the most rewarding. These methods are (i) look and say (or word-whole) methods; (ii) phonic method (by sounding single letters or groups of letters representing sounds (phonograms); or (iii) a sentence method (short simple sentences are read based upon the linguistic experience of the child. Easy recognition in varied contexts of words of not too great a perceptual difficulty marks the completion of this stage. The second stage comes at reading age of approximately six-and-a-half to eight-and-a-half years when the structure of unfamiliar words has to be analysed into phonic units and to be re-combined in an attempt to say the word. Most children, except perhaps the outstandingly able who may be unable to recall ever having to work through this stage, need some practice at phonic analysis and synthesis. When the phonic elements (PHONOGRAMS) are known and can be applied to analysing new words, the end of this stage is in sight. Examples of such phonograms are 'dr' and 'spr' at the beginning of words, 'ur' and 'ir' in the middle of words and word endings such as 'ing' and 'igh'. The third stage covers a reading age from approximately eight years to nine years and is a period of consolidation when knowledge gained in stage two is still precarious and needs reinforcement through practice with a variety of interesting reading material. Once a reading age of nine to ten years is reached, further reading progress seems to depend more on interest, attitude and practice rather than on a knowledge of the mechanics of the reading process. A reading skill at this level is unlikely to revert to an earlier stage, although reversion does happen if the skill is only in stage two.

There will be few school counsellors who will not meet at some time children and young people who have a reading disability, show other learning difficulties or who are underfunctioning seriously in reading skill. It is important for the school counsellor to know how reading skill develops, to be knowledgeable about remedial reading methods and to be aware of the need for the early detection of children with special educational needs. It has become increasingly apparent, during the last two decades at least, that many young people are capable of higher achievements if the effects of social, emotional and language handicaps can be remedied, or modified. It may happen occasionally that individual counselling may prove most rewarding if it takes the form of skilled help over a reading disability by the counsellor. Schools are increasingly concerned to organise remedial help on a systematic basis and the school counsellor will find it profitable to associate closely with the remedial department.

*The drive to achieve*

It is difficult to define the drive to achieve in orthodox terms as there are no useful objective measurements available. This concept seems to involve an awareness of a goal to be reached, combined with a willingness to exert maximum effort to reach it. There are several descriptive terms from everyday usage, such as industriousness, persistence, effort, desire to do well, determination to succeed, etc., which have over-lapping meanings. The drive to achieve seems to have much in common with the X-factor of the factor analysts; and Vernon (115) mentions that school marks appear to have a different structure from objective psychological tests because of this X-factor, 'a complex of personality traits, interests and background'. The school counsellor becomes interested in the conditions which prevent the formation of such a drive to achieve. Where such a drive is absent, it might be possible to apply remedial measures, although it does not follow that, knowing the reasons for underfunctioning, it will prove possible to counteract the conditions making for under-achieving. Some will prove resistant to change.

It was shown by Shouksmith and Taylor (88) that it was possible to have some success with high ability, under-achieving thirteen-year-olds by means of a simplified form of counselling offered by the teachers, although continued failure was experienced with some children. The factors making for success here appeared to be:

1. a warm, understanding, helpful relationship between the teacher and child carried on over a long period of time;
2. attention focused on a problem shared with an adult;
3. improvement in self-esteem of the children—they were considered important enough to receive concentrated personal attention;
4. an encouragement to change attitude towards academic work, possibly reinforced by a change of attitude by the parents towards the child.

There is little usable information from research which might help either in explaining why some children lack this 'drive' or in devising an environment which might create the conditions favourable to its growth. Where it is absent a myriad reasons for failure can be advanced—reasons connected with the personality of the parents, social class background, the nature of the home environment, the tone of the school environment, the degree of helpfulness shown by parents and teachers in supporting children through their growth problems, as well as the idiosyncracies of each personality. The Robbins report (42) records that many high ability students (mostly of working class origin) were leaving formal education at too early an age. The kind of linguistic background, and the values, expectations and attitudes which might lead to such working class under-achievement is one of the main problems needing solution.

Some suggestive hypotheses have been advanced by Bernstein (8) to try to account for known class differences in educational attainment. He describes two modes of speech linked with the lower working class and the middle class arising through the linguistic patterns evolved via the parents. Early childhood experience of a RESTRICTED CODE of language typical of the lower working class becomes a handicap when the young child tries to adapt to the ELABORATED CODE (typical of the middle class) prevalent in the educational system and regarded as essential if academic progress is to be made. Failure to adapt to such a code may inhibit new learning and the position within the social group can become progressively reduced. An attitude of antipathy towards school, and towards people who use the 'elaborated code' of language develops which emphasises difference and separateness. The child learns his position in the social structure and becomes increasingly resistant to the influence of the educated group. It is important for counsellors to be aware of these ideas in trying to communicate with some children and young people.

Lawton (60) analyses such factors in the interplay between education and class background and makes a plea in effect for the school environment to be more helpful to working class children either by introducing special educational and social measures in 'down town' schools or by matching more closely than at present the appropriateness of the schooling received to the kind of linguistic and domestic handicaps found. In some way effective communication between parents and schools must become a two-way process; on the one hand the parents must become more involved in the education of their children and on the other hand the school must understand, and compensate for, the linguistic and cultural handicaps of the home. How this may be achieved is one of the main problems for future research. The provision of special linguistic programmes in the early years at school, the employment of specially trained teachers and/or social workers and intensive studies via a multi-disciplinary approach have all been suggested (see Pedley 71). One warning, however, is necessary. The importance of social class background in influencing academic achievement cannot be doubted, but its influence may easily be over-estimated and other factors such as the personality of the parents (in terms, for example, of Eysenck's dimensions of personality such as tough-minded—tender-minded, or the normal-neurotic dimension) or the ideas parents have about child upbringing may be just as crucial, if not more so.

*Devising a school's testing programme*

The development of an adequate testing and assessment programme in the schools has been stressed by many writers. For example, Wiseman (131) stresses the need for such a programme, especially in secondary schools.

> The whole picture of our research underlines the need for an adequate system of educational guidance in the secondary school. By this is meant an organisation staffed by teachers trained in educational psychology and charged with the task of measuring and recording not only pupils' abilities and aptitudes, their scholastic strengths and weaknesses, but also their environmental handicaps and assets, their interests and ambitions, their outstanding traits of personality and temperament and their general development through the early years of adolescence.

The principles behind a testing programme are based on several assumptions. Any testing programme is only a part of a continuous process of assessment from the early years of schooling (age five) till young people leave school (at present fifteen to eighteen). Such continuous assessment is based partly on teachers' observations either in the form of a five point rating scale graded from A to E (no more complicated rating than this is necessary) on measures of effort (or drive to achieve), or temperamental traits or in the form of an order of merit when qualitative assessments are given in rating degrees of skill in any attainment area. An adequate system of recording needs to be available in the form, perhaps, of a school record card. Elaborate and complicated school records are sometimes suggested, but they are time-consuming to fill in and it is doubtful whether such complex records can contribute any more to assessment than can a much simpler and less time-consuming system. There is a clear need for a basic information card, which would act as a secretary's quick reference card. Then a single sheet is needed which summarises at a glance academic progress, personal information and scholastic history. Thirdly, a personal folder, or file, is necessary which might include all the bulkier material such as pen portraits by staff who know the student well, reports, letters, comments on standardised tests or special testing, and other detached papers of various kinds.

A comprehensive battery of tests should be planned for the age range eight to eighteen. Such a programme has a firm base in the primary school and ideally should cover intellectual, educational and personality assessment. Much variation is possible in the details of such a programme, but a suggested scheme is outlined in Appendix E.

*The assessment of interests*

Some attempt at the measurement of interest, attitude and of values can be useful for the counsellor as these are important aspects of personality, especially for the older age group. Such measures can frequently have a bearing on vocational aspirations. Any form of direct questioning to obtain information about a student's interests (especially those with vocational implications) are perhaps not very fruitful and there are large individual differences from an early age. Occasionally a young child seems to make up his mind as to his future occupation and works steadily over the years towards his goal, but such cases are relatively rare. Interests can fluctuate markedly, especially in the early years, but gradually some narrowing and crystallisation is observable. It is well known that ability and interest do not necessarily coincide. As the individual develops he gradually discovers himself and the constant re-shaping of interest patterns may eventually settle into a few broad outlines which can remain with an individual for a very long time indeed. The adolescent and young person has often insufficient information about occupational possibilities, new jobs are being created more rapidly than in the past, occupations change rapidly in content, style and nature. Thus the need is created for a means of approaching vocational interests indirectly and objectively. An interest test can sometimes serve as a useful basis for a counselling interview for the older person. The result of such testing can appear less threatening to the subject, rousing fewer anxieties, and seeming to have less emotional significance. Such testing appears more relevant to the world of work and its aims can perhaps be more easily understood. Two examples of such objective approaches in testing interests are (i) The Allport-Vernon-Lindsey Study of Values (2), and (ii) The Rothwell-Miller Interest Blank (RIB) (see Note 2). All these tests need special training before they can be used by teachers.

*Personality tests*

Effective personal functioning depends partly on emotional stability (i.e. freedom from the neuroticism dimension mentioned earlier) and partly on the realistic, original and creative qualities of thinking in everyday life. At the time of writing personality tests are only suitable for research purposes although eventually tests suitable for use by counsellors for measuring important aspects of personality may eventually be made available on lines similar to group ability and attainment tests. There is still a doubt, however, amongst experts as to whether personality tests are ever going to be capable of wide-spread application. Meanwhile the practising counsellor may have to rely on other instruments and methods. There are many practical as well as theoretical difficulties that have to be overcome in assessing qualities of behaviour, but perhaps the best judgements and assessments are the considered impressions of the experienced teacher who has observed a child's or student's behaviour and work over several months or years. Two instruments which have proved useful in helping to identify problem children who may need help are—(1) Stott's Bristol Social Adjustment Guides and, (2) Rutter's Children's Behaviour Questionnaire (Note 7).

Although the Stott guides are long and expensive, they are used extensively by teachers and have advantages in focusing in some detail on important areas in behaviour, in helping the newly-trained teacher to find out what to look for and in serving as a systematic form of interview for training purposes. However, as a screening device something shorter, cheaper and simpler on the lines of the Rutter Children's Behaviour Questionnaire is desirable. Tizard (108) analyses the virtues and defects of attempts at screening child populations for maladjustment and advocates a combination of a teacher's questionnaire and a parent's questionnaire to be used together for selecting children for further study. As an example of a teacher's questionnaire, Rutter's scale is short, easy to fill in and offers recent validation data. The scale consists of twenty-six brief statements of the kind 'not much liked by other children' or, 'often appears miserable, unhappy, tearful or distressed', and the teacher has to tick whether such statements 'certainly applies', 'applies somewhat' or 'doesn't apply'. A weighting of 2, 1 or 0 is given to each statement and the total score tends to pick out fairly effectively problem children from the rest. It also discriminates fairly accurately between neurotic children and anti-social children. This questionnaire needs to be supplemented by the parent questionnaire and by further observations from the teacher. Warburton (123) in a survey of personality testing applied to children observes:

> There is no particular reason, except conservatism, why certain objective personality tests should not be administered and scored by teachers in the same way that group intelligence tests are now administered and there would be the same need for adequate training in interpretation of the results. . . . It is not suggested, however, that this stage has yet been reached, or that it will be attained without a great deal more research and practical experience.

*Sociometry*

One of the more promising forms of assessment for the counsellor in schools is that associated with sociometric techniques. Basically sociometry is a method of recording interpersonal relationships within a group which has been together a long enough time to allow the separate members of the group to get to know each other well. Often the people we work with or live with can get to know sides of our nature which are often difficult to discover by the outside observer. Ratings of behaviour made by contemporaries (referred to as peer-ratings) often give useful information not easily arrived at in other ways. How this information may be used can be a delicate matter; those already feeling threatened by others in school or family may mis-use sociometric ratings quite unwittingly to impale the weak or to erect scapegoats. Peer descriptions of others can often point out an individual's characteristics which might hinder his acceptance by others. Such an individual may lack insight regarding his behaviour and some useful FEEDBACK may be a possibility in the counselling situation. The opinions of group members often influence others' actions and hence can partly determine the individual's subsequent inter-relationships within the group. An objective picture of the relationships and social structure of various groupings (such as classroom groupings) can be expressed sometimes in diagrammatic form, called a sociogram. Hierarchies of leadership, a 'pecking' order, and cliques can be identified as well as the most popular, and the social isolate. In such a way it can sometimes be possible to identify people who need special attention. Sociometric information may be used for assigning members to sub-groups or suggesting a reorganisation of a group with a view to better functioning or improving the effectiveness or morale of a group.

The choices made by group members must be seen to be genuine ones which result in action affecting the working of the group—the initial directions should always include reference to genuine group activities. To be assured of the confidential natures of the reports and to be made aware of the true purpose of the exercise is essential. The activities in which choice of companion could be offered may involve the formation of study and work groups or special committees, etc., and should always be within the experience of the members. Whatever precautions are taken, however, sociometric ratings can sometimes arouse anxieties especially amongst adolescent girls. For a more complete study of a group's social relationship it is sometimes held that rejections as well as the positive choices need to be made, but in the writer's opinion this is neither necessary nor desirable. Examples of the kind of questions asked in a sociometric investigation are: What do you like best to play (or play with) in the playground? Who do you like best to play with in the playground? What do you like best to do at your desk in the classroom? Who would you like best to have sitting near you in the classroom? At music or games time who do you like best to do things with or have sitting near you?

All degrees of sophistication are possible in formulating these questions and in analysing the results and a thorough analysis of sociometric data can become a very complicated affair indeed.

Such sophistication is mostly unnecessary as usually the most important information about the main patterns of social relationships can be obtained by simple counting. The information gained only applies to one group structured at one point in time. Over a large period of time social group structure can change and an individual's sociometric rating may vary between different groups. Other possible uses are to widen choices to be made outside the classroom and this can reveal interesting information, for example, about loyalties outside the school situation, although if no re-grouping follows from the choices this can alter the significance of the ratings made.

*The scientific problem—prediction and control*

For those working closely with people, a science of behaviour sometimes seems a long way off. The search for laws, regularities, uniformities and consistencies in behaviour is a worthy long-term aim, but there is little secure knowledge on which prediction and control of behaviour can be established at the moment. Clearly attempts at prediction can be made. For example, it can be stated fairly confidently that a thirteen-year-old with a Terman-Merril IQ of 165, under certain conditions, will do well academically at a university. These conditions, however, may not be present, in which case it might be possible to cultivate, create or control them in such a way that the prediction is still capable of fulfilment. In the absence of such control (and much behaviour in everyday life is not susceptible to such control) premature conclusions should be avoided and the wide limits of errors in prediction acknowledged. Slowly evidence might accumulate which might indicate possible ways of bringing such conditions eventually under control for predictions to be fulfilled. Respect for evidence, a willingness to submit to objective checks whenever possible, the necessity of revising one's models of the universe, and of people, all the while, and a realisation of the provisional nature of conclusions, are the essential qualities of a flexible scientific attitude. The knowledge gained from research is cumulative and perpetually revised in the light of further investigations, and the counsellor must be prepared wherever possible to incorporate into his practice the results of such research.

In all experimental work there is an attempt to control conditions in such a way that meaningful and predictable outcomes are possible. While in personal counselling there is an attempt to control the psychological processes, in the interview the ultimate aim is eventually to hand over our control when the ability to assume self-direction is demonstrated. Schools, too, are primarily concerned with the control of behaviour and the more predictable such behaviour can become, the more are the pupils defended against, and protected from, anxieties of various kinds. The aim of such control in schools is the same as in personal counselling, to be able to hand over such control to the individual so that their own behaviour becomes self-controlling and self-directing and can exist without the support of the institution or of other individuals.

## SUMMARY

There are three routes for gaining information about individuals; by observation, by introspection or by objective methods or experiment. Each area by itself is insufficient for adequate assessments.

Various objective methods are available for the counsellor in the form of objective group tests. Individual tests need special training and in any case are mostly irrelevant for the day-to-day work of the counsellor. Besides classifying tests into 'group' and 'individual' they can be classified according to the purpose intended: attainment tests, general ability tests, interest tests, personality tests, clinical tests and aptitude tests, the last two being of little relevance to the counsellor's work.

Testing is a complex matter demanding special training, and perhaps special abilities, on the part of the tester in test administration, scoring and interpretation. The counsellor should be aware, however, of the special features of a testing programme and of the kinds of question such a programme can or cannot answer satisfactorily.

An interest in under-achievement is one aspect of a counsellor's work. The problems arising from attempts to assess intelligence, reading skill and a drive to achieve are of concern to the counsellor who should understand the principles involved.

In the assessment of personality perhaps the most useful guide is the collation of teachers' opinions, or the use of sociometric ratings. The nature of interests becomes important from adolescence onwards, partly as a basis for interviews and partly because they are related intimately with occupational adjustment and vocational guidance.

Finally, research is important for checking on preconceived ideas and rigidities in thinking and in offering an opportunity to alter practice as well as to accumulate knowledge.

## NOTES

1. *Educational Guidance in Schools—standardised tests for the use of teachers* and the *Test Agency Catalogue* can be obtained from the Tests Division of the National Foundation for Educational Research (NFER), The Mere, Upton Park, Slough, Bucks. Information about tests is also contained in Buros, *Sixth Mental Measurements Yearbook*, The Gryphon Press, New Jersey, 1961.

2. Courses are available for teachers on testing and further information can be obtained either from the local education authority or from the Department of Education and Science. More specialised training is available on certain tests e.g. on the Morrisby Differential Test Battery or the Rothwell-Miller Interest Blank at the Independent Assessment and Research Centre, 5 Tavistock Place, London, W.C.1. The levels of qualification that are demanded of test purchasers are laid down in the front of the NFER *Test Agency Catalogue*.

3. For an account of some current individual tests see Vernon (114, pp.52-72) or the two compendious volumes on psychological testing by A. Anastasi, *Psychological Testing*, 2nd edition (Macmillan, New York 1961); or by L. J. Cronbach *Essentials of Psychological Testing* (Harper & Row, New York 1965).

4. The majority of clinical tests are not relevant to the counsellor but the student wishing to explore further can start profitably on C. E. Gathercole, *Assessment in Clinical Psychology* (Penguin Science of Behaviour, 1968) where a useful list of references is given.

5. This programmed reading material is American and consists of attractively prepared card material, graded according to reading level, and arranged in boxes (called laboratories) for ease of handling. The cards are carefully graded according to interest, age and to difficulty of vocabulary covering all reading levels from the beginning of reading to University level. Most children enjoy reading through this scheme and the occasional Americanisms in words and style are no hindrance. Further information can be obtained from S.R.A. Reading Laboratories, 11, Reading Road, Henley-on-Thames, Oxon.

6. A special class of reading disability labelled dyslexia with a neurological and physiological cause, has been suggested, but the evidence for such is inconclusive and still a matter of opinion (see D. Russell Davis and Asher Cashdan, 'Specific Dyslexia' p.80. *Br. J. Ed. Psych.*, Vol. 33. Pt. 1. February 1963).

7. See D. H. Stott, *Manual to the Bristol Social Adjustment Guides*, 2nd ed. (University of London Press, 1963) and M. A. Rutter, 'Children's Behaviour Questionnaire'. *J. Child Psychol. Psychiat.* 8, 1967.

## FURTHER READING

A clear, concise and readable account of the theoretical background in testing is given by Pidgeon (72) and a rather fuller, more detailed and recent text on the principles behind psychometric testing is in Pidgeon and Yates (73). More difficult texts are those by Vernon (114) and (115).

The best recent introduction to intelligence is by Butcher (16).

The literature on reading is large but probably the most easily available and profitable accounts are covered by (i) Keir (56); (ii) J. M. Morris, *Standards and Progress in Reading*, NFER 1966; (iii) J. Downing (ed.), *The First International Reading Symposium*, *Oxford* 1964, Cassell 1966; (iv) A. T. Ravenette, *Dimensions of Reading Difficulties*, Pergamon 1968; (v) V. Southgate and G. Roberts, *Reading—Which Approach?* ULP 1970; R. Gulliford, *Backwardness and Educational Failure*, NFER 1969.

The articles on 'Measurement of Personality' by Warburton (123) supplemented by Vernon (113) enable the student to go further into personality tests, the former a very readable introductory survey, the latter more difficult and wide ranging. Chapter 4 of Lovell (63) gives a bird's eye view of the field of personality and its measurement.

A lively and provocative but stimulating book offering views on human nature as well as on the testing movement, creative thought and the nature of research is by Hudson (49). For an analysis of the likely effects of social class on personal development see Lawton (60) for some interesting suggestions.

An early survey on interests by Wiegersman and Barr (126) gives many examples of tests that might be worth exploring as well as a theoretical background.

The best introductions to sociometry in this country are available in Evans (30), (31) and (32).

For those students interested in finding out about the relevance of research see 'Educational Research and the Teacher'—a report of a

Conference held in October 1965, at the Institute of Education, London University, or Wall, 'The Future of Educational Research' *Ed. Res.* Vol. 10. No. 3. June 1968 pp.163-169; or J. Anderson and A. H. Kerr, 'A check-list for evaluating Educational Research' *Ed.Res.* Vol. 2. No. 1. November 1968. pp. 24 and 75.

Those interested in planning small-scale research should read Evans (33) which is an excellent summary of basic information needed by the beginner in research.

# 5 Individual and Group Counselling

## INTERVIEWING

It was stated earlier (Chapter 4) that in order to appraise the behaviour of others three avenues of acquiring information must be explored—those of observation, introspection, and objective tests. Each is necessary for a balanced view in the assessment of people. The interview is a means of observing one small sample of behaviour, the deductions from which may, or may not, have relevance to the purpose in hand. There are many kinds of interview with different purposes according to the settings; and although we are primarily concerned here with a counselling interview in a school setting, there are universal features of interviews in industry, medicine, education and other fields which have some significance for the counsellor.

The interview is a 'special branch of the general art of conducting human relations' (Oldfield, 69). It becomes a form of creative thinking involving a reciprocal interchange of experiences, a reciprocal giving, and receiving, of feeling and attitude. It can be seen as a form of bargaining encounter between two people, each of whom may be willing to give something in exchange, the interviewer offering help, or a willing ear, the interviewee offering information, stating a problem and expecting advice, reassurance or sympathy. The interview becomes a form of personal relationship involving feelings of like or dislike, inspiring confidence, or leading to a lack of confidence in the other.

It is now generally accepted that the interview by itself is a highly inconsistent and unreliable means of predicting behaviour in the future, or for selecting people for particular jobs, or for diagnosing states of mind, or for assessing the nature of a personal problem as in marriage counselling. In selecting children for grammar schools, for example, the interview by itself with individual children is no longer regarded as making any contribution to the prediction of future academic success and has been abandoned by most local authorities. Research in other areas, too, has demonstrated time and again serious deficiencies in consistency and accuracy. The interview can sometimes offer important clues as to personal qualities, but different people interviewing regularly, all certain of their soundness of judgement, can frequently come to opposing conclusions. These conclusions seldom agree with the objective facts. For the school counsellor this is particularly important, as the picture built up of ability and personality in individual interviews may not be a correct or accurate one (see note 1). The counsellor must inevitably rely on others' observations to a considerable extent and be prepared to question his own views, as well as those of others, perpetually refining, adapting, reassessing and modifying his ideas as new evidence comes in. Errors of assessment occur with the most skilled interviewers and it may be that one of the most important differences between the more skilled and the less skilled lies not so much in the errors recorded as in the speed with which they are detected and corrected. The degree of self-deception in the interview is discussed by Eysenck (34):

> The interviewer becomes convinced that the picture he builds up of the interviewee's personality and ability is a correct one, and in the absence of any challenge to this opinion, and particularly in the absence of a follow-up procedure which will force him to pay attention to his numerous failures, the interviewer becomes more and more convinced of his God-like omniscience and ability. Time and time again does one encounter the individual who admits all the evidence about the inadequacy of the interview, but stoutly maintains that he or she is the one outstanding exception to this general rule, and that his or her opinions are almost invariably correct. (Needless to say, experimental studies of such individuals fail to disclose any greater ability to forcecast success and failure among them than is found among other people).

In spite of all these strictures, however, the interview is likely to remain as there is nothing to replace it—objective tests, or mechanical devices are unlikely to be effective, or acceptable, by themselves. The personal interview will remain, as now, an important part of the entry procedure into Universities and Colleges of Education as well as into all forms of industry and government. As Rodger suggests in his introduction to Sidney and Brown (89) the wise thing to do is not to disparage the interview but to try to improve it. The aim should be to study closely what occurs and to be aware of the individual's influence as well as his limitations.

Every interview reflects aspects of earlier relationships with similar persons and brings in both conscious and unconscious forces, rational and irrational. Two major processes stressed by the psychoanalysts here appear to be important. Transference denotes the process of transferring the emotion that the interviewee has previously felt for somebody else in his past life (most often with parents) on to the interviewer. In such a way hostility, aggression, over-dependence and over-anxiety can be displayed in the interview and the interviewer can be responded to as if he were the parents. Equally important, even if more difficult to recognise, is the process known as counter-transference. The interviewer responds to the interviewee as if he were somebody else; his own emotional needs interfere with the establishment of a relationship and can occasionally upset the balance or purpose of the interview. It seems possible that transference rarely occurs in first interviews and is more likely to appear in more prolonged interviews in a counselling relationship. These two processes occur in varying degrees in most people and perhaps form the basis of prejudices. Awareness of these prejudices does not necessarily make it possible to prevent their effects from appearing. One of the safeguards here against such prejudice, transference and counter-transference, is to have the support of colleagues in a team where frequent meetings and conferences illuminate relationship problems, and such help may cushion the effects. For the school counsellor it is important to have such mutually supporting help by frequent contact with other counsellors and by some organised system of continued supervision and in-service support after training.

The main attributes of a counselling interview lie in an exchange of feeling and attitude, not in an exchange of information, in answering questions, in offering solutions to problems or in giving advice. Oldfield (69) describes this 'fundamental process' as 'an exchange of attitude' and 'an encounter between two individuals in which there is mutual attitudinal reaction'. Communication will not be effective in any interview unless the atmosphere is warm, accepting and non-judging. The counsellor must be seen as non-threatening and must be prepared for occasional rejection. Sidney and Brown comment (89):

> An interviewer who is concerned to change attitudes will not make headway unless his work is based on the recognition that only secure people can risk change. Their confidence is based on past successes. Thus the interviewer will never achieve anything permanent if he threatens the bases of a person's security; sometimes his first task must be to do what he can to broaden and strengthen these bases.

Every interview involves an element of manipulation in the sense that the participants are trying to get something from each other. Initially at any rate their aims may not agree. It is very difficult (some think impossible) to keep personal values from the interview, as the interviewer must bring the other person into the right frame of mind for fruitful communication to take place. For example, initial aggression and hostility, if based on an underlying anxiety, will have to be dissipated first before progress can be made. Values and beliefs can quite unwittingly be foisted on to others and patterns of manipulation repeated without conscious intent. Oldfield (69) describes two kinds of 'attitude manipulation', the diagnostic and the therapeutic, and he considers that interviewers should attempt to distinguish clearly between the two. In diagnostic manipulation the interviewer's own feelings, attitudes, values, are dominant in trying to provide situations in which reactions can be released. The interviewer 'deliberately provides the occasion for certain attitudes to be displayed'. The purpose is to allow the other to reveal his feelings about a wide range of topics in order to build up a picture of the interviewee—a deliberately contrived attempt to find out what the other person is like as a person. In the therapeutic form of manipulation, changes are desired in specific attitudes, or habit systems, or in self-image and 'this is one object of attitude-manipulation in psychotherapy'. In counselling, too, such manipulation can be observable whether the technique is based on a largely authoritative, directive, counsellor-centred method or on the permissive, non-authoritarian, client-centred method. From the point of view of technique in counselling it may be that the counsellor would use all methods directive or non-directive, likely to achieve his aim.

In recent years studies have been made of ways of processing information derived from a knowledge of communications engineering (called CYBERNETICS). From these studies the interview can be seen as a form of communication, as a system of sending and receiving messages. The sender (interviewer) must encode information by processing it into symbols and signs that are understandable to the receiver (interviewee), who must then decode it. Breakdowns, errors, disturbances, interruptions will occur, and an analysis of the reasons for failure to recognise the signs, symbols and assumptions of the other can become very complex. A much used term, 'feedback', is used to describe the ability of SERVO-MECHANISMS to control and govern themselves. The effects of one person's behaviour on the other enables feedback to take place, leading to modification of behaviour. Failure to get feedback means inevitably ineffective communication; those skilled in receiving feedback know themselves well, through their effect on others, and are able to communicate more effectively with others. Great individual variation is possible—the rigid thinking, insensitive and hard-to-condition person may not be capable of feedback and such people remain unmodifiable.

At the present time there are no ways of inducing change in some people's attitudes, prejudices or beliefs. Many attempts have been made to modify certain problem families, often with little success. It is important to remember too, that the skills the interviewee uses in dealing with other people are valuable to him as they are the best he has been able to devise. The poorer or the fewer these skills are the more he is liable to hold on to them. Sidney and Brown (89) observe in commenting on the rigid thinking person:

> Thus an interviewer will observe the paradox that people whose attitudes seem to have brought them little success, will most strongly

resist any evidence that these attitudes need adapting. Many failures will have convinced them, not that their responses are inadequate, but that they must cling to the responses that have brought what little acceptance they have managed to gain.

On social skill training courses, some can often be helped in self-awareness by being given feedback about their shortcomings.

The physical conditions of interviews are important. They are part of the whole process of making people at ease and of ensuring a calm, unhurried, unstrained atmosphere. While the quality of the relationships in the interview is far more important than the physical setting, yet no one can deny that physical comfort (easy chairs), privacy, an attractive and pleasant room, and freedom from distraction are essential.

## THE NATURE OF INDIVIDUAL COUNSELLING

The counselling interview shares the disadvantages of interviewing in general. It differs from other interviews in having primarily a therapeutic purpose and is conceived as a way of establishing a helping relationship. The counselling process is probably as old as history, although only in this century has it taken on a new meaning for an old practice. As M. Jourdain discovered in Molière's *Le Bourgeois Gentilhomme* that he had been talking prose all his life, so there will be some readers who will discover for the first time that they have been counselling without knowing it. Although I am concerned here with counselling in schools, there are elements common to all counselling anywhere, although there are specific aspects that only apply to certain fields. (See Appendix B for an account of counselling in other fields.)

Definitions have their limitations as well as virtues. It is not possible to gain understanding of such a complex process as counselling within a single definition and it can be misleading in the sense that distorted ideas may occur in the absence of long and detailed explanations. At the risk of such misunderstanding it might prove helpful to those who derive benefit from a definition to repeat the one offered elsewhere (105). Individual counselling in schools can be defined as a way of 'offering an opportunity to the young person' to experience, 'a one-to-one relationship which is accepting and tolerant yet relatively free from moralising, directing, advising or judging'. In this way the hope is that enough understanding will be gained of themselves 'so that they can stand on their own feet without support'. The key features of such a definition are 'offering an opportunity' and, wherever possible, counselling interviews should be seen as voluntary, to be able to be ended at any time or started up at any time by the client, and freely available to all. No attempt should be made to enforce attendance even if this were always possible. 'A one-to-one relationship'—this should be seen and felt to be private and confidential, with defined time limits and regular appointments. 'Accepting and tolerant'—the tone of such interviews should be seen and felt to be relaxing and non-threatening. 'Enough understanding'—this entails an attempt to alter the self-image and to answer questions such as 'Who am I?' 'What do others think of me?' 'What do I think of others?' 'What am I like as a person?' 'How able am I?' 'What do I wish to become and how can I reach my goal?'

'Standing on their own feet without support'—this is one of the aims of all education and of personal development. It implies that some young people need to be dependent on a sympathetic adult over a period of time and that learning to be independent is a gradual process to be approached unhurriedly and in easy stages.

Some of the basic characteristics of counselling are outlined by F. Roberts (76) in a description of a two-year experiment in school counselling in a London Comprehensive School of 1,800 boys. He mentions the five qualities which enabled him to establish a helping relationship with select groups and individuals as (i) acceptance; (ii) listening; (iii) responding; (iv) empathy; and (v) trust. The stress throughout the counselling was on feelings, attitudes and emotions and not on fact-finding or the giving or receiving of information or the seeking of solutions to problems. Help could be achieved through a personal relationship with a 'therapeutic personality'. Such a personality is not that of an expert, or adviser, or an authority (although the counsellor within the school setting must willy-nilly be associated in the eyes of some young people with the 'authority' surrounding all aspects of school life).

'Acceptance' he defines as 'receiving the person as he is without making a judgement on his behaviour or feelings'. This implies being able to enter into the client's world, or 'frame of reference', an ability on the part of the counsellor to see the world as the other person sees it. There are degrees of effectiveness in communication here—there may be unintended rejection on the part of the counsellor (to love the unlovable is often a tall undertaking). He may be more involved in putting across his own thinking rather than attempting to follow the client's thinking. Some cannot respond to the permissive attitude of a counsellor either because they are not ready for face-to-face talks, or perhaps they expect either punishment or a very authoritarian approach (expecting to be told what to do). The child or young person from an authoritarian and hostile home background can present quite a problem here and if there is anti-social behaviour of an extreme kind within the school, such counselling may not be possible or very rewarding. It assumes an ability on the part of the child to see the counsellor as warm, understanding, sincere, interested, concerned, trustworthy and non-threatening. This is difficult sometimes to achieve in a school setting, but certainly not impossible. The core here is an accepting attitude on the part of the counsellor. 'The relationship develops naturally and spontaneously and becomes a reality to the individual as the counselling sessions progress' (76, p.207).

Next Roberts notes 'listening' as a vital part of the counselling process—such listening is an active and creative process, not passive or 'wooden'—the focus is on feelings rather than on content—on how something is said rather than on what is said. The interpretation of non-verbal clues mentioned earlier are important—facial and postural as well as verbal clues, mannerisms and silences. Listening demands perpetual vigilance and patience and continual attention to the nature of the dialogue between counsellor and client. As a form of creative thinking, listening is a high level skill where the application of rules or of a pre-determined plan is not always possible. The effort to attend and to search for significant patterns can be exhausting, as many counsellors can testify. 'Responding' means responding with understanding, not casually or haphazardly—'such understanding coming through a combination of sensitivity (a personal quality) and interpretive skill (a technical ability).' Again, the counsellor's personality is important here—not only must he have the right ability and educational background, but he must be the kind of person young people like to talk to. The age of the counsellor is probably of less importance than is commonly supposed, as the so-called generation gap can be so easily bridged by some of the older generation. The young counsellor may initially appear to get a quick and more immediate response, but provided 'old' counsellors have the 'right' personality, age seems to be no handicap.

Great variation is possible in the kinds of personality that make for successful counselling. Semeonoff (85) carried out a psychological study for the Scottish Marriage Guidance Council in the years 1953-1955, when selection conferences extending over two days employed procedures modelled closely on the leaderless group techniques used by the British War Office Selection Boards (WOSB) when selecting potential army officers for training. He mentions that:

(a) fairly clearly defined stereotype of the counsellor personality undoubtedly exists . . . a person who is sensitive to personal relationships, aware yet tolerant of human failings (including his own), able to recognise contrasted points of view, to inspire confidence and, on a slightly different plane, one who has made a sufficiently stable adjustment to his own life situation.

The ability to listen, and to respond, in Roberts' sense then, is a key feature in the counsellor's personality although it is easier to be more certain of undesirable qualities that make for ineffective counselling than to be too definite about the positive qualities making for effective counselling. The counsellor should have a high degree of personal security, self-acceptance, self-awareness, and be relatively free from the need to be liked, and approved of, by everyone or to depend on others for supporting his ideas. He must be able to steer a stable course between a mature, concerned involvement with young people with personal social and emotional difficulties and yet at the same time be capable of detachment and non-involvement when necessary. He should be relatively free from disabling anxiety and be able to avoid over-identification with the young person and to be able to see people as mainly a product of feeling and emotion, rather than as logical and rational. He must tolerate ambiguity and contradictory tendencies in himself as well as others without resort to fight, flight or panic.

These personal qualities are important in Roberts' fourth point of empathy: 'If the counsellor's interpretation of what the person is trying to convey is correct then he "feels" that we understand him'. Such 'understanding' may come about through awareness that someone is prepared to take a personal interest in him, and that he is being accepted and respected as a person in his own right. Rogers describes this as unconditional positive regard. Often to be respected by someone else is the beginning of respect for oneself. Part of this process is achieved through trust on the part of the person being counselled.

> It makes all the difference to him to find someone who really understands his underlying feelings. He is encouraged, therefore, to reveal more and more about the actual feelings which have contributed towards the emotional conflict. On the basis of a new found trust here, with the counsellor, this experience can be generalised to other personal relationships, so that the old pattern breaks down under the new learning.

Before this position of trust can be established it may be important that the interviews are seen and felt to be private and confidential and this is no easy matter, especially for the older child or adolescent. The latter will often have their own ideas as to whom they can, or cannot, trust and they will seek to identify their own 'counsellor', preferring perhaps the housemaster or other teacher within the school, in which case the school counsellor will be there in a supportive role if needed (note 3). Reference outside the school may be preferred by the adolescent and this could be arranged by the school.

From the discussion so far, there appear sufficient similarities between counselling and psychotherapy to make it easy to confuse the two and it is important for the school counsellor to be aware of the divergence in method and function. The setting obviously influences function; the school counsellor in school is available to deal with all children and where there are problems these mostly fall within the normal range. The counsellor is not aiming for personality change but is more concerned to accept the other as he is rather than as he ought to be, and to establish a helping relationship which stresses the need to use whatever resources are available for dealing with the world as he (the client) sees it. A psychotherapist functions mainly, but not exclusively, in a hospital or clinic setting and sees his clients only after psychiatric diagnosis. Occasionally psychotherapists work in ordinary schools and perhaps only the acute shortage of trained personnel prevents an extension of their work in schools. Psychotherapists also work in special schools for maladjusted children, both day and boarding. These clients need an intensive, highly skilled and prolonged approach and nearly always have severe personality problems. In a psychotherapist's training his cases are supervised regularly by medical and non-medical experts. The training is long and arduous and includes a personal analysis. The school counsellor does not deal with too seriously disturbed personalities, although he should know when, or how, to refer to others when such cases come his way.

There is much to learn from the psychotherapist's approach that may have relevance and use within the school. There are always dangers in offering rules which can appear to oversimplify complex problems, but some find it helpful to have a few guidelines which may serve as a basis for discussion. Writing in the psychiatric field, Professor D. Russell Davis outlines a possible scheme in his *Ten Rules for Therapists* (24). These are:

1. He is impartial and does not take sides with or against the patient in the complaint he makes about the behaviour of others.

2. He respects the patient's obligation to decide for himself and to act on his own behalf and thus recognises the patient's full responsibility. He does nothing to limit the patient's control over his own situation.

3. He divests himself of authority and power, and especially the power to change the realities of the patient's situation, except perhaps in a few trivial respects.

4. He affirms the patient's fellowship of the community.

5. He acknowledges the laws, rules, customs and conventions of the community.

6. He respects the confidentiality of what he is told.

7. He does not allow the patient to make unnecessary disclosures about others.

8. He listens, says little and keeps his own experience out of it.

9. He avoids facile re-assurances which deny the patient's distress or the seriousness of the situation as the patient sees it.

10. He keeps interpretations to a minimum. Questions are more helpful than assertions. If they are offered at all, explanations are expressed in terms of circumstances rather than motive.

There are quite striking overlaps here with counselling and these rules can be extended with profit to counselling in schools. *Impartiality* is important as it happens that children and young people try to get the counsellor on their side by making specific allegations or complaints against members of staff or other children. It is important for school staff to realise that such a rule holds in all counselling sessions and applies equally well to complaints against the school counsellor, members of staff and others. To break this rule can mean becoming involved often quite unintentionally in another's emotional problems. An over-identification on the part of the counsellor with the child and against the teachers and parents is a danger in school counselling. To take sides is not good counselling.

It is important that the client's capacity for *self-direction* is respected on all occasions. In counselling the young person has every right to make his own decisions, although obviously, as everybody knows in schools, some younger children are not always capable of such self-direction—limits and boundaries have to be drawn by the school, as well as occasionally by the counsellor. With most adolescents perhaps the best attitude to take is that of a kindly but firm and consistent authority—a frank, open, definite, matter-of-fact approach. In counselling students in a College of Education, Ingleby (51) refers to the 'need sometimes to be more directive in counselling young people' and the need for 'an adult who will function in a substitute parent role'. To respect the other's right to make decisions is a good rule for the counsellor to adopt provided such decisions are based on the best information available, that the counsellor is aware of the implication of these decisions and that haste and impulsive action are absent. Freedom of choice is possible, too, as long as the freedom of other individuals is not too much affected.

*The absence of omnipotence* is an all pervading characteristic of counselling. Many come to the counsellor with expectation of magic to be performed, or expecting to be told what to do, or seeking a quick solution to a personal problem. Satisfying these desires can be a serious bar to effective counselling as it may prevent the counsellor from acting as a catalyst or mirror for changing the self-image of the counsellee. All the resources of the *community*, both within the smaller context of the school and occasionally in the wider context of the community outside the school are available. Ingleby (51) stresses this point:

> The student counsellor, or the school counsellor, is working within the context of a smaller community; one which broadly speaking reflects society, but which also has a life of its own. The counsellor is a part of this life; if he is to carry out his work he has to be accepted into this community and adapt himself to its special needs. A major part of his work must in the beginning be concerned with enabling the group as a whole to understand what he is trying to do, and also adapting himself to what the rest of the group is trying to achieve. The two are not always compatible and the most obvious example is when the student he is counselling is falling short of the requirements of his colleagues. The counsellor has somehow to enable the student to recognise the situation he is in and at the same time to appreciate the student's difficulties—without on the one hand asking them to put up with what may be to them an intolerable situation, or on the other hand requiring the student to conform to a state of affairs with which he cannot cope.

The counsellor works within a structure and except in a few small details this cannot be changed. School children have to adapt to this structure and except for occasional truants and school refusers there is no opportunity for opting out. Rules and conventions, in the design of which they have had no part, must be accepted.

Some of the difficulties and dangers in school counselling are now apparent. Too seriously disturbed children may be taken on for counselling where they might need a different approach with a different background of training. Unaware of his personal limitations, and feeling perhaps rather too keenly committed to help all those in need, the counsellor may be emboldened to help the unhelpable. Adolescents with severe behaviour problems showing in out-of-school behaviour are particularly difficult to deal with by counselling within the school. On the other hand, some interesting developments in ordinary schools—in group counselling for example—might be possible in the future and in which the school counsellor could be involved.

Emotionally deprived children must be approached with considerable caution by the counsellor. Such children are often searching for a relationship and can make for the inexperienced counsellor a superficially agreeable, quick and apparently effective, emotional contact. They may have a rather desperate need to be accepted and understood and often attempt to make relationships with any who offer sympathy and affection. If such a relationship is started up by the school counsellor within the day school setting it may well not be possible to control this constructively or effectively. To have to break such a relationship may mean further damage to the young person, reinforcing perhaps previous rejections by adults in the past. A residential setting rather than a day school setting may lead to easier control and where the needs for a long term relationship with an adult can be more easily satisfied. Lees (61) comments that some have difficulty in accepting 'the degree of damage suffered by the child or the parents which perhaps cannot be rectified by a good environment or even by other help available'. She notices 'a tendency to struggle to keep a child with his family, almost at all costs, however damaging this may appear just so long as the child has not committed some offence that brings him before the Court'. The severely anti-social cannot always be helped in a day-school setting, or even occasionally in a maladjusted day school. The need for punishment or for an authoritarian approach may make any attempt at a permissive approach to be construed as weakness and there may not be the right conditions available for this to be worked through. One other danger needs to be noted here. The counsellor through regular interviews may gain insight into the reasons for his client's behaviour and may be able to work out an apparently neat and nicely formulated pattern of explanation. It is not always appreciated that it is both pointless, and possibly damaging, to try to share this new found knowledge with the client by attempting to make him conscious of the reasons for his behaviour. It may be necessary to wait often for a considerable period of time, until he arrives at such knowledge himself. If and when he does so it may be more helpful then to discuss the implications of this insight with him.

## GROUP COUNSELLING

Much of our knowledge about people seems to have come not from laboratory experiments so much as from a study of people in real life situations, or from the creative artist. In particular, the novelist and dramatist contribute greatly to an understanding of the interplay of motives in the family and in society at large. There is a whole field of experience here which the diligent counsellor might cultivate with profit and only a passing reference to the influence of literature can be made here (see note 4).

A systematic study of groups by the social scientist is still only in the beginning stages although perhaps enough is known for the counsellor interested in this field to make some tentative probings. Man is a social animal and social concepts are necessary for a description and explanation of the multifarious groupings that take place from birth onwards. Any adequate description of a person always seems to involve placing him in a group setting, family, school, church, social class and so on. Often the ability in adulthood to join satisfactorily in groups is conditioned by the early experiences with a variety of groups in home and school, the immediate family (parents) and the extended family (relatives).

A study of group behaviour shows that every person is like every other person in a few ways, in other ways he is like just a few others, while in still other ways he is uniquely different from everybody else. Groups of various kinds can be seen as ways of exposing these similarities and differences and of expressing their uniqueness in a social setting. It is a truism to assert that there is enormous variation in behaviour, and in value and belief systems between different cultures, national groupings (of class or race) although it is widely known that the differences within each grouping are greater than differences between groupings. Nowhere is this more in evidence than in school groupings (in the classroom as well as in other national groups) which are used primarily to facilitate learning. They can often seem wasteful of time and effort unless the group has a strong attraction to its members. A sense of loyalty, or of belonging, is necessary for these groups to function well. Some individuals have no desire for group membership and this has to be respected. The paradox has been observed many a time where sometimes the highly sociable may be capable of prolonged periods of withdrawal from social contacts and in no sense need this be regarded as either strange or abnormal. The interest in people and in group functioning may be that of the relatively uninvolved scientific observer rather than that of the emotionally involved participant.

Malfunctioning in groups can occur if there are too few, or too many, group members for the purpose. The optimum size for group counselling seems to vary between six and eight, whereas a lecture in a large secondary school can be effective with a group of over 100. The purpose of the grouping must be clearly stated and generally realised by all the members. Considerable skill and effort is needed to form and maintain successful groups, just putting people together is not enough. The group can be dominated (and sometimes wrecked) by one or two unsuitable members. It may be possible to contrive their exclusion before the group is formed or by forming a special therapeutic group. Group leaders may fail to bring out the best in other group members, either by over-autocratic methods or by not offering enough opportunity for adequate and meaningful discussion.

There are many other reasons for group failure and it is important for the school counsellor to be aware of the reasons why certain groups fall apart or become disorganised so that the principles governing effective groups can be used for establishing counselling groups. The purpose of these groups can be either to discuss personal relationships generally or, with older students especially, to study their own behaviour. An attempt might be made to help children and adolescents understand their emotional problems in a group setting. These groups must not be started by the experimentally-minded amateur since special training, special skills and intense preparation are necessary before they can be introduced into a school or elsewhere. Richardson (75) outlined her methods of forming special groups of students in a Department of Education where they met regularly for the purpose of each group studying its own behaviour. Although this was a stimulating and worthwhile opportunity for intending teachers to understand their emotional conflicts in relation to one another, yet she warns against teachers attempting such study groups in schools as the teacher

> would need a great deal more preparation for the role of consultant than could be provided by membership of one adult study group . . . the development of techniques for conducting adolescent study groups in the institutional setting of the secondary school may itself be a field for future research projects.

D. Cartwright (18, pp.388-391) summarising research on techniques of achieving change in people by means of groups offers eight principles as a guide to those working with groups:

1. If the group is to be used effectively as a medium of change, those people who are to be changed and those who are to exert influence for change must have a strong sense of belonging to the same group.
2. The more attractive the group is to its members, the greater is the influence that the group can exert on its members.
3. In attempts to change attitudes, values or behaviour the more relevant they are to the basis of attraction to the group, the greater will be the influence that the group can exert upon them.
4. The greater the prestige of a group member in the eyes of the other members, the greater the influence he can exert.
5. Efforts to change individuals or sub-parts of a group which, if successful, would have the result of making them deviate from the norms of the group, will encounter strong resistance.
6. Strong pressure for changes in the group can be established by creating a shared perception by members of the need for change, thus making the source of pressure for change lie within the group.
7. Information relating to the need for change, plans for change and consequences of change must be shared by all relevant people in the group.
8. Changes in one part of a group produce strain in other related parts which can be reduced only by eliminating the change or by bringing about re-adjustment in the related parts.

The aims of individual counselling can also be realised in group counselling. In both the main aim is to help each individual achieve a more positive and realistic self-image. The self-concept has been receiving much attention in recent research work and was discussed in an earlier chapter (p.57). It is regarded by many (cf. Rogers) as a vital part of personality having a deep and lasting effect on behaviour. It has been defined in various ways; Zahran (136) defines it as: 'an organised, learned, cognitive and unitary configuration of conscious perceptions, conceptions and evaluations by the individual of his Self as he actually is (Perceived-Self), as others are supposed to see him (Other-Self), and as he would most like to be (Ideal-Self)'. Such self-concepts develop as a response to social pressures acting on 'the inner drive to Self-maintenance'. It is commonly believed that though there is a tendency for these self-concepts to remain consistent, they can under certain conditions be changed. Rogers (82, p.189) maintains, for example, that 'when a person's view of himself changes, his behaviour changes accordingly'. Zahran in his research tried to show that it was possible to measure these self-concepts by means of various objective tests which he carried out on a group of 170 secondary modern adolescents (aged thirteen to fifteen) and that such measures might be of great use to the school counsellor. They might be used, for example, to identify children for group counselling, for selecting for these groups and for measuring any changes that could occur during group counselling.

It is important to distinguish group therapy from group counselling, the differences being similar to those obtaining between psychotherapy and individual counselling. In group counselling in schools an opportunity is offered to young people for immediate and direct contact in specially selected groups where hostile and negative feelings can be expressed to each other in such a way that the personal growth of individuals within the group can be furthered. In this way it is hoped that feedback can take place with resultant change in the self-image. In group counselling it is possible for some members to accept those ideas from their contemporaries which may well have been rejected if made by adults. To find themselves accepted by their peers with all their faults can be reassuring showing, as it does, that the differences between themselves and others is not so great perhaps as they had imagined. To realise that others have problems too can offer a relief for some from anxiety.

The school setting is in many ways ideal for group counselling; it is more natural and less artificial than individual counselling. The latter certainly seems inappropriate for some young people who may respond better in a group. The group might offer greater personal security for some, but for others the fear of ridicule or of being rejected by their peers may make individual counselling more attractive. Group counselling can be a transition stage to individual counselling once the counsellor's image is established as someone who is available for help if needed. Some may need to experience an individual relationship before they become capable of relating to others in a group. Those already receiving individual help outside the school (such as attendance with Probation Officer or at a Child Guidance Clinic) as well as those already being counselled, should perhaps not be placed in these groups. Still others may be too shy and nervous of talking in front of adults or even of their peers. They may not be ready for, nor have any wish to be involved in, group counselling. Any attempt at enforcement is likely to prove ineffective and attendance must be seen, and felt, to be voluntary.

The principles of group counselling in schools have still to be worked out in detail and the whole field lies open for systematic study. Perhaps these groups must ensure a degree of homogeneity in emotional maturity, levels of intelligence and attainments, while at the same time excluding the difficult personality problems. The latter should certainly happen if the counsellor has any doubts about his success in being able to cope with such problems. But all this is uncertain and conjectural. Success or skill in dealing with classroom or other natural groupings is no guide to likely success with counselling groups because the purpose and skills required are so very different. There is perhaps less control possible over counselling groups than over classes. Certain kinds of confidential information cannot be discussed in a group. In those whose psychological defences are fragile, too much might be revealed in a group that could conceivably lead to embarrassment in the school where they still have to face their companions in a school setting. And this can be especially embarrassing for the older teenager. It seems then that limits and boundaries must be drawn, realised, understood and accepted by all members. Even with trained and highly skilled counsellors the starting of counselling groups within the school should be approached with caution and try-outs with selected pupils who appear capable of responding well may be necessary first.

## SUMMARY

Everyone recognises the limitations of interviews, although they are likely to remain the main avenue of communication acceptable to most people to achieve a variety of purposes. Certainly techniques of interviewing are basic to school counselling. Continued attempts need to be made by interviewers, of widely differing levels of skill, to offset the effects of the interview's fallibility by understanding the psychological processes occurring in the interview.

For the school counsellor there are two main purposes; diagnostic (defining the problem) and therapeutic (offering a helping-sharing relationship). These two purposes can merge, but the counsellor must be aware of their separate functions. Several psychological processes must be understood, even though it may not always be possible to do anything constructive about them oneself, e.g. transference and counter-transference phenomena (together with other 'mental mechanisms') need to be appreciated. It may be possible to counteract their effects to a small degree if colleagues are available, preferably from different disciplines, for extended discussions. In special social skill training courses feedback from others may help awareness of personal deficiencies.

Individual counselling is a highly skilled task whereby the counsellor offers a therapeutic relationship to aid the personal growth of another person. How this may take place or what the personal characteristics needed in a successful counsellor may be is not known with any great certainty. But the counselling interview must be seen by the counsellee as non-threatening, basically non-authoritarian, non-advice-giving, always available if needed, voluntary and private and confidential. The counsellor should be available to all, but not forced on all. School counselling (both group and individual) is different from psychotherapy although the similarities lead to some common principles.

Group counselling can be seen as a skilled form of helping relationship although the starting up of group counselling methods in schools (secondary schools especially) is only at the beginning stage. In schools group counselling, skilfully conducted, may be effective in promoting personal growth on lines similar to individual counselling—namely changes in the self-image leading to desirable changes in behaviour. The school setting is probably ideal in developing these procedures and the future may see much experimentation here. Special training, a high degree of skill and systematic study is necessary before sound progress can be made beyond the very tentative.

## NOTES

1. This applies to all interviews; the psychologist, for example, has always two basic questions to answer from each interview: (i) How reliable are my observations likely to be? To what extent are they likely to be repeatable or to be consistent? What factors in the other, as well as in oneself, appear to be making for unreliability? (ii) How valid are my observations? How well do they agree with other observers? If there is no agreement, to what may this be due?

2. W. Trotter made this point in *Instincts of the Herd in War and Peace* (ed. R. W. Chapman, O.U.P. 1953): 'To suppose that when one has admitted the liability to prejudice one can free oneself from it by a direct voluntary effort is a common belief and an entirely fallacious one. Such a task is far beyond the powers of the most fully instructed mind and is not lightly to be undertaken except by those who have least chance of success'.

3. The whole process of keeping counselling records is a complicated one and is very much linked with trust and confidence. If counselling records are kept, they should be separate from the cumulative records discussed previously in Chapter 4. It is arguable whether any special records of counselling sessions within the school should be kept without the client's knowledge and consent, or even whether such records are necessary (cf. Holden, 48, who argues against the practice of keeping detailed records). If detailed records are maintained they should be regarded as specific to the counsellor and to no one else and should always be used in such a way that safeguards the privacy and integrity of the individual.

4. For those wishing to explore this theme further, David Holbrook's books (*English for Maturity*, 2nd Edition 1967, or *The Exploring Word*, Cambridge University Press 1967) or M. L. Hourd's books (*The Education of the Poetic Spirit* or *Coming into Their Own*) or

any good modern novel such as A. Sillitoe's *The Loneliness of the Long Distance Runner*, Salinger's *Catcher in the Rye* or Golding's *Lord of the Flies* will provide ample material for extending experience about human relationships. In drama, for example, Arnold Wesker's *Roots*. Many other examples can be sought by the literary minded.

## FURTHER READING

Oldfield (69) and Sidney and Brown (89) are probably the best initial guides to the interview. The former was a study made from watching many interviewers at work in a variety of situations, some many years ago; the latter was written mainly with a view to industrial and occupational interviewing.

Roger's views on individuals have already been mentioned in Chapter 3. This can be supplemented by Boy and Pine (12), Stewart and Warnath (95) or by the various short articles appearing in *Marriage Guidance* or *The New Era*. A recent British view on the teacher's view of counselling is Holden (48) while Wallis (122), although writing specifically on marriage, has much of relevance on the nature of counselling. On the nature of groups generally in schools although of marginal relevance to group counselling, see B. Kaye and I. Rogers, *Group Work in Secondary Schools and the Training of Teachers in its Methods* (O.U.P. 1968) or K. M. Evans, 'Group Methods', *Ed. Res.* pp. 44-50. Vol. 9, No. 1. November 1966. M. L. J. Abercrombie's 'Small Groups' in Brian Foss (ed.), *New Horizons in Psychology* (Penguin 1966) introduces the reader to most of the current literature on small group theory.

Probably the best introductions to group counselling are by Richardson (75), and by Stewart and Warnath (96). K. A. Williams' short article 'Group Counselling', *The New Era*. Vol. 51, No. 3, March 1970, makes some useful points.

# 6 Families and the Counselling of Children with Special Needs

## COUNSELLING OF CHILDREN WITH SPECIAL NEEDS

It is important that the school counsellor should know something of the structure and function of the family, the wide variation in family patterns, and how family relationships influence the young person's development. The differences in family patterns both within a culture and between cultures are considerable, and this has led some writers such as E. Bott (10) to doubt whether efforts at classifying families are worthwhile. She concludes 'that it is impossible to make general, universally applicable assessments of levels of family functioning . . . the standard is arbitrary . . . and many families will not subscribe to it'. It is always difficult to know what is happening to personal relationships in the family when emotionally involved from the inside and it is almost as difficult for an outside observer. Many professional workers of varying expertise can be called upon to advise on family problems, and all realise that systematic study of the pattern of relationships in the family is as important as knowledge of what is going on in any particular individual member of the family.

When there are disturbances in family relationships, it often helps if someone emotionally uninvolved can look at the family objectively. Bott and her co-workers found how difficult it was, however, trying to chase this myth of objectivity. They developed ways and means of reducing subjectivity and emotional involvement by frequent contact with colleagues from varying disciplines, in this way trying to combine psychoanalytic (e.g. transference and counter-transference) and sociological concepts.

We were working on the assumption . . . that a person's feelings towards other people will be determined not only by what the other person is really like, but also by patterns of perception and feeling built up through past experiences with people who were emotionally important. (Bott, 10, p.42).

Family structure and function is known by most people from their own experiences and there can be few who do not have an image of the normal, happy, healthy family. Such an image is a personal one, based on prejudice and opinion, and the concept of 'normal' is arbitrary and ambiguous. There are many ways in which family patterns, and roles within the family, are supposed to be changing. It is often assumed that the world trend is towards monogamy and greater equality between man and wife; that families are becoming more child-centred than adult-centred; that there is more psychological freedom for children and that there is generally a relaxation of parental discipline. Other assumptions that are sometimes made are that the *rules* governing the family are changing: the man is no longer head of the household and responsibility for discipline and all other aspects of family life should be shared. *Belief systems* are supposed to be changing—the belief that woman's place is in the home is changing to a belief in the interchangeability of male and female roles. It is also said that *values* are changing—'the essential purpose of marriage is the procreation of children' becomes 'marriage is a partnership between equals, where sex is a cultivated pleasure and contraception widely accepted as a means of controlling number and timing of children'.

There is little evidence, however, that can be produced in support of these views or of the alleged decline or improvement in the quality of family life. If family patterns are changing this could be due to:

(*a*) the widespread use of technological invention—e.g. television and motor car;

(*b*) the increased geographical mobility of families, with the immediate family becoming less dependent on the extended family;

(*c*) greater longevity with the resultant increase in the numbers of old folk as well as the length of working life;

(*d*) the widespread acceptance of the idea of family limitation;

(*e*) the continued decrease in infant mortality;

(*f*) the tendency for married women to work outside the home;

(*g*) the earlier age at marriage.

How these changes are affecting family life will continue to be a matter for speculation. The few attempts to approach a study of family functioning objectively have come up against immense difficulties in definition, in method, in selection and in interpretation. These difficulties are outlined in Bott's study (10), which is a recent attempt to get at the facts of family life by studying twenty ordinary families in their homes. She suggests a possible classification of family organisation on the basis of the husband's and wife's role within the immediate family (husband, wife and children). Families could be classified according to three types of organisation:

1. the complementary organisation, where the husband's and wife's activities were separate and different, but where they fitted together to form a whole;

2. the independent organisation where their activities were carried out separately without any reference to each other;

3. and the joint organisation where they carried out their activities together although this did not exclude some activities being carried out separately by either partner at different times. The role relationships in these organisations were determined, she thought, by the network of social relationships existing outside the family. These could be either loose-knit (i.e. few such relationships) or close-knit (i.e. many such relationships).

There were many variations possible between these two extremes. At one extreme there was the family showing a high degree of segregation (the independent organisation) in role relationship where the husband and wife had a close-knit network where many friends, relatives and neighbours knew one another. If the partners come from such a close-knit family network and this can be continued after marriage (the marriage being superimposed on these relationships) the outside activities will continue to be influential on the family. At the other extreme there were families that had a joint role relationship (joint organisation family) and a loose-knit network of social relationships (few relatives, neighbours or friends knew each other).

If husband and wife come to the marriage with loose-knit networks, or if their networks became, after marriage, loose-knit, they must seek in each other some of the emotional satisfaction and help with familiar tasks that couples in close-knit networks get from outsiders. Joint organisation becomes more necessary for the success of the family as an enterprise. (10, p.60).

Bott's study indicates that marriages showing extreme differences in pattern are able to bring up happy children, and can be rated as contented and happy marriages. The sharing of roles, or the carrying out of joint activities are neither better nor worse than rigidly segregated roles, where the father is out every evening, in pubs or elsewhere, attends his social groups or appears to lead a very separate existence, leaving the wife to the domestic chores and to receive emotional support from neighbours, relatives and friends. Many of the families in Bott's sample were in a transitional state between these two extremes and were moving from one kind of network to another.

Young and Willmott (135) found in their survey of East London families a close-knit network imposed on marriages where husband and wife roles inside and outside the family were rigidly segregated and where the three-generation mum-centred family is still powerful in some of the older industrial areas. The married daughters remained closely dependent on mum and the husband spent most of his leisure time away from home. These relationship patterns can change, however, when the immediate family moves to new housing estates (and where inevitably there are feeble links with the community). Close ties with mum are weakened and the organisation of the family changes to a joint or co-operative one, each seeking in the other the support that was not needed so much in the past.

Another kind of classification of families was offered by Carter (17) and used by him in his study of secondary modern school leavers in spite of the well-known pitfalls in such classifications. To classify his families (who were mostly, but not exclusively, working class) into three main types, was useful in his investigation, as each type tended to have a different influence on the children who were preparing to leave school and go to work. Firstly, there was the 'home-centred aspiring type' of family (which he further sub-divided into the 'traditionally respectable' and 'newly affluent'); such a family is small in size, and 'independence and respectability' are the key features. There is a strong desire to maintain material and behaviour standards and everything is done 'for the children'.

Discussion is a normal part of home life in these home-centred families: there is no embarrassment in exchanging views and information—whereas in many working class homes serious topics are rarely raised, and, when they are, there is awkwardness because of a lack of facility in expression and because of an inability to rally information and to draw rational conclusions. But in the home-centred families the ability to plan ahead and to think things out is reflected in daily conversation. (Carter, 17, p.43).

The next type of family Carter considers is the solid working class type, which is seen to be on the whole easy going in most things, taking life as it comes; there is little pressure for academic achievement and the lack of parental ambition borders on inertia. The concern is not to fall in the social scale rather than to show any ambition for rising, and the conditions of life are accepted unquestioningly. The family is less of a cohesive whole than the home-centred family; there is less working together on the part of the parents. It is the mother who is the central figure in this household. It is the mother

who makes such plans as are essential—budgeting to meet the gas bill, for example, or arranging for the window to be repaired. She manages the house—her husband's role is to earn the money, and, having done this, he expects, and his wife regards it as proper, that the home will be run for him. It is rare for husband and wife even to discuss affairs of the household, whether it be on small matters of the colour for new curtains or whether on more important subjects, such as the sort of job the son should aim at. Anything to do with the kids is the mother's business. It is she who writes notes to school, or goes along to see the teacher if called to do so. In some families, indeed, the father deliberately refuses to get involved in affairs affecting his children. The latter may take this for granted, but they may be bitter, as the comment of one boy shows: 'My old man didn't even put down the bloody paper to listen. He didn't even bother to hear what I was saying. It's been like that for years'. (17, p.52).

The picture here is typical of Bott's type of family where rigid role segregation is allied to a close-knit network. There is less emphasis in these homes on privacy and frequent contact is made with neighbours, relatives and friends. The language used in this type of home is reminiscent of Bernstein's (7) restricted code where the more involved grammatical structures are missing, imperatives and interjections are more frequent and there appears a failure to conceptualise adequately. (See chapter 3).

The third kind of family Carter describes is that of the 'rough, deprived and under-privileged'. These families appear to have little truck with society's conventional values or traditional moral sanctions. The values shared are often those of a 'delinquent sub-culture'—there is much feeling for themselves as a group against the rest of society. Conventional organisations are spurned and they see no point in conventional moral values such as honesty, or considering others before self, unless these are related to their own cultural group. Success in society has no meaning for them (it is 'us' against 'them'), the law and middle-class values are often rejected. The father often changes jobs which are usually of the unskilled or semi-skilled variety. If and when wages are high the money is mostly spent on their own pleasures. Families are larger and the children receive little consistent training; babies arrive in quick succession, and there follows material, linguistic and emotional deprivation. Emotions are very near to the surface in these homes and the early family experiences continue to be a handicap throughout life and to pre-dispose the children to social breakdown. These families

. . . repudiate the values of the school and have as few dealings with the teachers as possible. Truancy is not unusual, whilst children are kept away for trivial reasons—or allowed to indulge in their desire to stay away. Children couldn't care less about what goes on at school—it is an unwelcome infringement upon liberty: it may be positively hated, and the teachers and all they stand for scorned. What do they know about life? There is no affection for learning, no appreciation that joy may be derived from lessons. (17, p.58).

Considerable information about problem families is collected by certain statutory and voluntary social welfare agencies (EWOs, CCO, schools, etc.), but this information is likely to deal with only relatively isolated aspects of a family and not with the family as a whole. Attempts to integrate these approaches are likely to increase with the partial implementation of the Seebohm report (42) by the Local Authority Social Services Act, 1970, which recommends an integrated social work department covering all social workers. Efforts to achieve integration were being made in some local authorities before legislation, e.g. Lees (61) who, together with her colleagues in Hounslow, tried such integration as a means of improving communication between schools, EWOs, other social workers and the Child Guidance clinic. It was found that there was often failure to appreciate the varying needs of different kinds of family and how these could be met by different social agencies. She found it helpful to distinguish five types of family pattern:

1. the delinquent and anti-social (this corresponds with Carter's 'rough, deprived and under-privileged' family);
2. the multiple problem family with psychotic parents (such parents showing an abnormal or pathological mental state constituting a definite disease entity);
3. the concerned but inarticulate family whose children often have problems, mainly with the school, where children often show the characteristics of the slow learner;
4. the concerned family with emotional problems probably responsive to less intensive casework help; and
5. the family of the school phobic child.

Although Lees gives no expanded definitions of these types of family, such a scheme has obvious utility.

It is often difficult to help the anti-social or delinquent family by using present methods. Large numbers of young people are likely to continue to need placement away from home in Approved Schools (Community Homes) (see note 1) and it is generally recognised that problem families often cannot be helped by a voluntary approach characteristic of many social services (e.g. Child Guidance facilities). They are often unable to understand such an approach ('What's the point of just talking?'). They will interpret any intervention as a threat to their autonomy, or they will fail to see the need for any modification of the family pattern. This resistance to change is characteristic of most families, but applies particularly to those under discussion (see note 2).

We have already seen some of the characteristics of the anti-social family from Carter's (17) description of the 'rough, deprived and under-privileged' family. The under-privileged sections of society often congregate into so-called 'delinquency areas' in our cities and appear to belong to their own, often delinquent, sub-culture. They are basically non-conforming, have little respect for property, and law-breaking can be a way of life for them. To the outside observer the lack of ethical standards appears part of the family tradition where anti-social attitudes are handed down directly to succeeding generations; there appears little appreciation of the need to train children in consistent and acceptable patterns of behaviour and schools try to devise an educational routine which can compensate for these handicaps. Often the children appear to be given unlimited freedom from parental supervision encouraging gang behaviour. Children from these families are often emotionally deprived and the ability to make satisfying relationships is impaired or broken because of damage or breakdown suffered at crucial stages in personal development. Jones (54, p.34) comments:

lower working class children are more often deprived of maternal love than their middle-class counterparts. The baby is always made much of, petted, dressed up, and shown off. But as families are large, a child is soon displaced from this favoured position by a younger rival, who also then proceeds for a very brief spell, to monopolise all the attention of his mother. Each child in turn, without the preliminary 'hardening off' through social training, which a middle-class child would have received, is dispatched to the company of his brothers and sisters, and so becomes very dependent upon them for acceptance and love. This sudden and almost brutal separation from his mother seems likely to have its effect upon a child's sense of values . . . (he) is flung in at the deep end . . . anger and resentment are likely consequences; but he also seems to grow up with what is often inaccurately called 'a weak character, i.e. weak inner controls, because he has been given no time or opportunity to develop anything stronger. Impulsive behaviour, often destructive and hostile, and almost infantile in character, results from such deficiencies in the ego. He is under constant inner stress, as weak inhibitions and restraints seek to maintain their tenuous control over powerful and unintegrated interests—and often fail to do so.

## PARENTS AND COUNSELLING

The diversity of family pattern so far described is much greater than might be suggested by these rough-and-ready classifications and many schools have been concerned during recent years to respond to such diversity by creating a variety of formal and informal links between the home and school. These arrangements can range from formal parent-teacher associations, meeting regularly for joint activities between school and home; and special appointments systems for parents to see teachers for regular discussion of their children's problems; to the appointment of specially trained social workers to the school staff whose main function is to support the efforts of both school and home to further the personal development of each child. Occasionally teachers themselves, who may have a special interest in developing contacts with the home, may be involved in home visiting. This can occasionally be a fruitful way of co-operating with a school counsellor involved in personal counselling. Sometimes, however, children prefer to keep the two parts of their life, school and home, in separate compartments and this must be respected. It is nearly always unwise for the counsellor, who has built up a special relationship with the child to become involved with the parents or family as this relationship may easily be damaged. Holden (48) in a similar situation preferred to involve a teacher colleague in the family, while Roberts (76) when involved in counselling the child preferred the form tutor to see the parents. 'Parents will too easily manipulate personal meetings with the counsellor to their own advantage and this is soon indicated by a deteriorating relationship with the boy'.

It is now accepted that parents need to be more intimately involved in their children's schools than ever before. Stern (94) outlines the varying practices adopted in approaching parents in different countries. Parental care can be seen as an educational problem and it follows that schools are likely to become more involved in preparing young people for family life and parenthood. In schools where the main aim is to foster good human relationships they are likely to be involved in a more systematic approach to parent education. As Stern (94, p.11) observes: 'converging trends of thought in child psychology, psychoanalysis, social psychology, social anthropology, and psychopathology have contributed to an increasing emphasis on the importance of parents in the mental development of their children'. It is not enough to think in terms of giving more information by lectures, courses, or through the formalised channels of a parent-teacher association or to think in terms of a 'school' for parents on the lines of formalised instruction. The majority of the parent population will not be reached this way, formal offers of help will have a restricted appeal, and will apply only to the occasional individual. Informal groups, where the principles of group counselling and social casework are combined, are likely in the long run to be more effective and more acceptable, as this would take into account the personalities involved and the parents' differing opinions, attitudes and experiences. In such a way, too, the approach to the children's education through the parents' education might become more meaningful and effective than at present.

Several attempts have been made recently to involve parents closely in education on these lines. Kellmer Pringle (57) described some parent group discussions which were started up at the suggestion of a parent who wondered whether a meeting could be arranged 'just talking'. Groups of parents varying in size from ten to eighteen and two members of staff were involved in 2½-hour meetings (the optimum length of time was considered to be about 1½ hours to 2 hours). The main discussions centred around three topics:

1. how special treatment for children worked and why it was that children enjoyed going to special classes and yet talked little about it to the parents;

2. various problems arising in the rearing of children;

3. the causes of different educational difficulties. Kellmer Pringle noticed that 'parents taught each other to appreciate the various problems from a different point of view'. (57, p.134).

This method has similarities to that described by Slavson (92) who used group discussion with parents as a form of group counselling, to further their understanding of their relationships with their children.

> Parents who have faced the inevitable difficulties of child rearing and parent-child tensions are helped to understand feelingly the plight of the child, as well as their own as parents. They are encouraged and helped to evolve attitudes, and take steps that decrease the unhealthy elements in parent-child relations and to free their children towards wholesome growth and personality integration, at the same time making their own lot less fraught with hardships and guilt.

Schools are in an excellent position to offer parents who are finding difficulty in relating satisfactorily to their children an opportunity to discuss their own childhood frustrations. They can relate their personality and family pattern to their failure to give their children opportunities for self-expression and normal development. These parents can often see parenthood as a means of satisfying their own psychological needs rather than as a means of assisting the next generation in their growth towards maturity.

In order to introduce a counselling system into a school it is important to make sure that all parents are aware of the purpose and methods of this system. The methods used will vary from school to school but there should be little difficulty in gaining the support of the majority of parents for any individual counselling of their children. Where difficulties arise and there is a breakdown in school-home communication, fear, anxiety, hostility and aggression are likely to be shown. When this happens and continues without change, individual counselling can be difficult and sometimes hazardous. As in any educational experience it is wasteful and ineffective if parents remain hostile and indifferent and it is ethically very doubtful whether the counsellor ought to intervene with any member of the family without their co-operation and consent. There may be ways other than personal counselling that may be available for dealing with these problems.

When dealing with children showing particular forms of linguistic, social and emotional handicap it is wise to seek an appraisal of the family before counselling takes place. This can be done either through the school social worker (if there is one) or through a member of the teaching staff who has the interest and special talent for making and maintaining fruitful school-home contacts. These contacts are particularly important for special groups of children—the delinquent, the maladjusted or the anti-social—who are likely to come from families already well known to, and involved with, social agencies outside the school. Close co-operation between the counsellor and these agencies is necessary to achieve effective co-ordination and to avoid duplicating responsibilities. The counsellor must be aware too of the special counselling problems that are thrown up by these families.

## COUNSELLING CHILDREN WITH SPECIAL NEEDS

School counselling, although available to all, is neither needed by everyone nor should it be necessary for the school counsellor to interview everyone in the school. His effective functioning here depends on the kind and level of skills available amongst the school staff and how he selects suitable clients. Aware of his strengths and personal limitations, he can screen for reference elsewhere; for help within the school, using resources in the staff and school organisation, and outside the school, by being in touch with different forms of professional help. Within the school he will know the key features of particular groups of children and their personal and educational needs—the slow learner, the gifted, the inarticulate, the maladjusted, the school refuser, those with reading disability and many other forms of social and linguistic handicap. Of these children two kinds are likely to engage his attention, the maladjusted and the school refuser, the former may amount to as much as a fifth of the school population, the latter (including truants as well as school phobics) only a very small proportion. Both are likely to involve much counselling time. As with the typing or classification of families, so the typing and classification of children has its limitations. Classifying people can often be for administrative convenience rather than as a psychological or scientific process, and this applies particularly to the maladjusted child. This category is an administrative one and its widespread use stems from its being a form of handicap for which local authorities are empowered to make special provision as one of the categories of handicap mentioned in the 1944 Education Act. Although psychologically not a very meaningful term, it is still generally accepted as having some use. Administratively the category maladjusted is reserved for children and young people who have been ascertained as maladjusted by a local authority procedure which includes an agreed assessment by a psychiatrist, an educational psychologist, a teacher and a psychiatric social worker for the purpose of providing specialised help. It is common knowledge that the number of maladjusted children is much greater than those officially 'ascertained'. There are maladjusted children in all kinds of school, special as well as ordinary, who are never ascertained and there are considerable numbers of children with other forms of handicap who could be classified as maladjusted (see chapter 1). A child or young person with a problem can be helped in several ways. He can come to the notice of the Probation Officer and be placed on probation or sent to an Approved School (Community Home). He can be helped by the Child Guidance Service and recommended for a day or boarding school for maladjusted children, or be given psychological treatment at the Child Guidance Centre. He can come under the care of the Children's Officer. Which of these services is used seems to be often largely a matter of chance. There is an overlap of the different kinds of maladjustment and no pure form is recognised—the maladjusted merge into the delinquent, the delinquent into the severely anti-social, the aggressive neurotic into the withdrawn, nervous neurotic, the school phobic into the truant.

The Underwood report (42), which looked at the whole field of educational and medical provision for maladjusted children, found that it was impossible to define maladjustment with any precision. This report noted, however, that 'even if it proves impossible to define maladjustment at all closely nobody can doubt that maladjustment exists'. Any definition may exclude the numerous, if less serious, cases of mild personality disturbance that every teacher comes across in school. (Note 4).

If maladjustment mainly arises from environmental stress then school must play a vital part in modifying the environment and in providing relief or containment of unsettled and disturbed personalities. There are some mild signs of maladjustment in school children which are transitory, and the school counsellor is one of the key helpers here. There is rarely one single cause of maladjusted behaviour but more often many causes acting together. Yet invariably present are disturbed relationships between parent and child. Bowlby (11) and others have emphasised the importance of the quality of the relationship between mother and child, especially in the early stages of development, the importance of a warm, affectionate, consistent relationship without disruption. Others have noticed the importance of the father/child relationship for normal development, e.g. Andry (1) and Taconis (101) stress that the father is important for providing a model for identification. Taconis makes a plea for more father figures in the early stages of the primary school and especially in infant schools. The differences in sex-roles seem to be diminishing and there is greater interchangeability of role between father and mother—(many fathers can take over the maternal role in child rearing while many mothers can take on the father's role by providing a substantial contribution to the family exchequer).

In his study of Approved School boys Stott (97) outlines cases where faulty parental relationships interfered with a child's development; and faulty father-child relationship was a prominent factor in his final analysis of causes of delinquency. From his work with delinquents he developed many ideas for counteracting the emotional deprivations of young people in their family life (Stott, 98). These were based on the belief that much human maladjustment could be prevented. He assumed two main principles behind human behaviour.

Every human being . . . requires to attach himself to a small, and, as far as possible, permanent group who feel warmly towards each other and in which he is accepted without question. Anyone without such a firm human anchorage is an unsettled, unhappy, potentially dangerous person; he may try to forget his anxieties in reckless excitement, or let them break out in open resentment; or as a defence against his unhappiness he may habituate himself to becoming an inhuman, unfeeling person who will have no compunction about doing injury to others. To the child his family is this belonging group . . . if he is obviously unhappy, restless or resentful then he feels his position within his family group to be insecure.

In other words, every child or young person needs to feel himself a valued and accepted part of a family group without conditions. In emotionally deprived children (who may be living with parents, be illegitimate, or have step-parents or a foster parent) the childhood environment fails them and breakdown occurs. If the parent or parents are rejecting in their attitude, or lacking in affection or sympathy, or have very little emotional contact with the child, conditions are established for anti-social behaviour with aggressive feelings directed against the world. If the parents are inflexible in attitude, over-punitive and hyper-critical, over-authoritarian, or more inconsistent than usual, it follows that anxiety states, feelings of inferiority, and shy, worrying, withdrawn, conflict-ridden behaviour in the children may result.

The second major human need mentioned by Stott centres around

> . . . the feeling of counting for something, having some status or being able to do things . . . if the child feels that his parents have no real interest in him, or put their own interests first to the extent that he is left to fend for himself; or if they are quite prepared to place him in other care, then he is likely to come to the conclusion that in their eyes—the people on whose opinion he places the greatest value—he is a person of no consequence. He develops acute inferiority feelings. This may mean that he will seize every opportunity of asserting himself, even though it may land him in trouble. Alternatively, he may become so discouraged that he never tries to do anything; his inferiority feelings may not show themselves in any behaviour of the inferiority-compensatory type (such as bragging, showing off and bravado) but when he imagines himself insulted he may flare up in a vicious temper and do someone injury.

Stott maintains that where behaviour and emotional difficulties are in evidence, then one or both of these primary human needs are being frustrated, i.e. there is no secure membership of a family group and the child does not feel a valued enough member of such a group. Stott emphasises, too, the potential contribution of the school in the early detection of behaviour problems and in preventing and modifying such behaviour. (Note 5).

The school counsellor may be involved with unsettled children at a number of levels. He would be involved at the diagnostic level within the school while defining the problems and appraising their significance in terms of the individual, the family and the school and drawing on school staff and specialists outside the school if necessary. After this appraisal, agreement is needed as to how to tackle the problem; whether or not an approach needs to be made to the home; who is the most appropriate person to make it and how this should be carried out. Occasionally maladjusted children return from boarding schools (Note 6) and have to be integrated into a day school. This is often an intricate and delicate process involving Child Guidance workers, family and boarding school staff. Sometimes children leave day maladjusted school to attempt partial integration with normal school children (perhaps for two half or two full days initially) with full integration taking place after a time. More day schools for maladjusted children are coming into being and close co-operation between the various schools is essential. One of the central aims of such special schools is to ensure a return of the child to the ordinary school community as soon as they are ready. The aim in these schools, both day and boarding, is to provide an informally structured therapeutic community in which concentrated attention can be paid to the promotion of the emotional growth of children and adolescents.

Although it is perhaps meaningless to talk in terms of success in this work, from some recent investigations there is evidence of the effectiveness of such special education. For example, Roe (79) applied objective measurements to a boarding school population and found improvement in a number of aspects of personality, such as reduced anxiety, sounder personal adjustment, less severe emotional disturbance. The reasons for sending children to these schools in the first place were connected with the quality of personal relationships at home; the child's emotional state; the risk of the child becoming delinquent, or being at risk in the community; the inflexible attitudes of the parents; their inability to control the child; or their failure to co-operate with the Child Guidance Service. If a return home proves feasible, the school counsellor will be involved as one of the team ensuring as smooth a transition as possible to the day school.

There is a long-established tradition of compulsory education in this country stemming from the 1870 Education Act. It has been estimated that over the country as a whole about ten per cent of children fail to attend school (cf. M. J. Tyerman, 109) although there is no sure way of gauging the accuracy of these estimates. Some reasons for failure to attend are physical illness, a deliberately contrived withholding by parents, truancy and school phobia. The last two are often associated under the general term, school refusal, the true extent of which is probably unknown as there appears tremendous variation from area to area in the way records are maintained. The distinction often drawn between the truant and the school phobic child is that the former largely starts non-attending on his own initiative, possibly without the school or home knowing about it initially. He has usually little constructive support from the parents, who may be negligent, or indifferent about maintaining continuous attendance. Truancy may be spasmodic or persistent, if spasmodic then the present activities of the EWO are usually sufficient for regular attendance to be resumed. Persistent truancy, however, either with or without parental collusion, will be for personal or social reasons, evading the parents as well as the school. Stott's studies (99) of the early boyhoods of his Approved School population indicated that truancy was one of the indications of a personality problem and part of the behaviour pattern which included wandering, running away from home, restlessness and gross over-activity. Tyerman (109) considers that all children frequently absent from school should be systematically examined as they are all in need of psychological help, although appropriate treatment will vary with each child's problems. He regards truancy as a sign of maladjustment needing special provision and attention.

> If a child is to develop a correct sense of what is right and wrong, he must have a warm and satisfying relation with an adult of good standards . . . it is essential for him to feel that he belongs to a group, that the members of the group feel warmly towards each other and towards him and that their standards of behaviour are socially accept-

able. The knowledge that he is loved and will never be forsaken gives a child confidence and freedom from anxiety. Only about one truant in four experiences this warmth and as a result the capacity of most truants to form good relations is probably greatly diminished or absent.

Although some recent studies doubt the value of a concept of school phobia, others hold that there is a different psychological basis between truancy and school phobia. In the latter the parents appear to be more involved emotionally in the child, who may show acute anxiety, bordering on panic when needing to leave home for school. These children often refuse to leave home, or, as in the case of younger children, run home from school during the day. Any attempt at a forceful solution is often quite out of place, as acute distress is often experienced. They do not engage in anti-social acts and often are quite content to remain at home. Many social and medical agencies may be involved with these children and it is often a matter of chance which agency becomes first involved until psychological help is finally provided by the child guidance service. In her survey of school refusal Cooper (21) quoted evidence to show that school phobia is a clinical variant of separation anxiety (often about separating from the mother) which itself is an indication of a much wider personality disturbance.

### THE COUNSELLOR AND THE CLIENT

One of the more interesting aspects of a book on counselling is a summary of case histories, but the reader must do without these on this occasion. Even if it were possible to work out a disguise so complete that clients could not recognise themselves, I have not been able to obtain their permission to make public the private side of their lives. The material obtained in individual counselling is private to the counsellor and client. Such an absolute rule occasions little difficulty, even where matters are revealed which may be said to involve the public interest (such as stealing), as it is always possible for the client to work towards taking appropriate action on his own account if the counselling is felt to be supporting enough. No difficulty arises within the school setting where good communication exists between staff and counsellor, as all will tacitly assume the importance of this confidentiality. (Note 7).

It is widely accepted that counselling cannot be learned from books alone (or from reading potted case histories); it is more an attitude of mind than a set of rules that can be learned and calls for qualities similar to those of the creative artist as much as for the systematic analysis of the scientist. Kellmer Pringle (in Halmos, 46) underlines this point in her discussion of some of the problems arising from attempts to teach personality development; 'psychological insight is not easily gained from textbooks and from lectures, but grows from first hand, practical and guided experience in which the whole personality is involved'. Such an attitude of mind is implicit in much of our present-day thinking in schools, as well as in counselling, 'an attitude of mind which accepts that sympathy and detachment, intuition and logical thinking, hypothesis and established fact are not only compatible but necessary'.

## SUMMARY

Any comparative studies of family life are difficult to carry out objectively and any classification of families must always be regarded as very tentative and provisional. The study of the individual in isolation from the family is not possible—although counselling help to individuals is often of indirect help to families. By helping one member of a family it sometimes is possible to influence the whole pattern of relationships within the family. Knowledge of the immediate and extended family is necessary for adequate appraisal. The extent of variation in normal family patterns is greater than is often realised. That there are changes in family patterns—in parent roles, in value and belief systems and in rules—is not in doubt, although the nature of these changes is bound to be speculative. It is impossible to produce evidence in favour of the decline of the family as an institution and it is more than likely that the immediate family will continue to be the basic and preferred unit in organised Western society. Personal relationships within the family are probably much as they have ever been.

It may be helpful for the school counsellor to type the family background in spite of the dangers of such labelling. Some agreed scheme of family classification is useful in order to match the appropriate form of help to the needs of the family. Family patterns are extraordinarily resistant to change, but modifications may occur by searching for ways of making families more secure and accepted within the school setting. One way is by having a team based on teacher— social worker—school counsellor. To approach the education of children through the education of parents (by group or therapeutic counselling) offers some hope of progress and advance in dealing with social and emotional problems.

Parents need all the help and support that can be contrived by the school and they will mostly welcome the help of the counsellor with their children. Although the counsellor will be available to see young people at any time in the school yet if prolonged personal counselling takes place within the school the parents must always be consulted first and their co-operation gained.

Two special groups of children are likely to take up much of the counsellor's time, the disturbed personality and the school-refusing child.

## NOTES

1. I have already discussed (p.53, Note 3) changes planned from the new 1969 Children and Young Persons Act. The Approved School will in future be named Community Home. Children's Regional Planning Committees (twelve are proposed to cover the whole of England and Wales) are set up under the Act to work out the kinds of facilities needed by young people in care in their areas and to plan observation and assessment centres. It may well be that new homes and hostels will be created so that children and young people can continue to go to their own schools while residing away from their families, yet sufficiently near to them to maintain constant contact with them.

2. An interesting description of a problem family is given by N. Hazell in Pedley (71). She indicates how a social case worker might become an effective helping agent (p.117).

3. A recent article by M. Chazan ('Maladjusted Pupils: Trends in Post-War Theory and Practice', *Ed. Res.* Vol. VI No. 1, November 1963) outlines the various definitions of maladjustment and concludes 'there seems little reason for changing a term which now covers such a wide variety of psychological conditions'—it is a useful umbrella term which 'gives the widest possible scope for appropriate help to be given to children in need of it'.

4. Even if the Summerfield Report (42) recommendation for a large increase in numbers of local education authority psychologists is implemented (the target is one psychologist for 10,000 children) this will still not cover the need for counselling services to deal with individual problems within each large school unit. (*Psychologists in Education Services*, HMSO 1968).

5. Classrooms which offer a chance to work through some emotional problems are becoming more common; *cf* a recent account by a teacher of a permissive approach to instruction and control of behaviour with a class of dull, disturbed and difficult ten year olds. (*And Softly Teach*, Achievements in Teaching No. 3 by the Research Committee of the Institute and Faculty of Education, University of Newcastle-on-Tyne 1967.)

6. There are many easily accessible accounts of boarding schools for maladjusted children. See for example, R. Balbernie, *Residential Work with Children*, Pergamon 1966, or the Department of Education & Science pamphlet, *The Education of Maladjusted Children*, HMSO 1965. For day schools perhaps the best recent account is by S. K. Bailey, *The Day School for Maladjusted Children*, Trends in Education, HMSO 1967, or *Day Schools for Maladjusted Children*, the Association of Workers for Maladjusted Children 1970.

7. Dr N. Malleson, *A Handbook on British Student Health Services* (Pitman Medical 1965), is unequivocally explicit on problems of confidentiality and such a view must be held, and seen to be held, by school counsellors if their prime task is personal counselling. 'Confidentiality . . . must be repeatedly made explicit in written material about the service, in orientation talks to teachers . . . and individually . . . Often the teaching staff might find certain information obtained from the students helpful, and if such disclosure might also prove helpful to the student then most of the counselled students give their consent for discussion with appropriate staff members. But where such authorisation is withheld (by the Student) this decision must be respected totally, and must be seen to be respected'.

## FURTHER READING

Bott (10), Carter (17) and Craft *et. al.* (23) supplemented by E. Younghusband (ed.), *Social Work with Families* Publication No. 4 of the National Institute for Social Work Training, are probably the best introductions to families. Still relevant, although written a long time ago, is J. C. Flugel *The Psycho-analytic Study of the Family* (Hogarth

1939). Stern (94), Slavson (92) and Kellmer Pringle (57) each throw different light on parent education. The Government pamphlet on Parent/Teacher Relations (70) offers useful points. Taconis (101) and Bowlby (11) complement each other in defining the parental role.

Books on maladjusted children have been already mentioned in Note 6. Stott (99), Cooper (21) and Tyerman (109) give most of the current views on school refusal. J. H. Khan and J. Nursten *Unwillingly to School* (Pergamon 1964), offers a Child Guidance approach to school refusal.

# Glossary

AFFECTIVE The adjective from AFFECTION which is a general term for the emotional or feeling aspect of mental experience.

CONDITIONING A process whereby a response comes to be made to a stimulus (or group of stimuli) different from that to which it is the usual response.

CYBERNETICS The study of human control functions, and of mechanical and electrical systems designed to replace them.

DENIAL A 'defence mechanism' whereby people refuse to admit to painful experiences or to painful aspects of themselves.

ECLECTICISM A mode of approach to experience or knowledge which does not follow one system or theory, but which selects, or uses, what are considered the best elements of all systems and theories.

ELABORATED CODE A system of language habits which are characteristic of a 'middle-class' mode of speech where complex grammatical structures are used linked with a belief in the virtue of systematic language training.

EXTRAVERSION—INTROVERSION A dimension of personality now associated with Eysenck's work and according to which all individuals can be placed at some point along a continuum between these two extremes. The extravert has interests directed outwards towards nature and towards other people ('outgoingness') while the introvert has interests directed 'inwards' to the thoughts and feelings of the self ('introspective').

FACTOR ANALYSIS A statistical and mathematical analysis of objective test results which confirms or refutes hypotheses regarding 'factors' as determinants of physical and mental performance.

FEEDBACK Originally a term from cybernetics it is now used as a synonym for the knowledge of the results of any behaviour which influences, or modifies, further performances.

INTROJECTION In psycho-analysis the process of absorbing into the personality other persons—a form of identification. For example, the super-ego part of the mind is formed by the introjection of parental figures.

NEUROTICISM—NORMALITY Another Eysenckian dimension of personality. The neurotic is to be distinguished from the healthy and normal individual by showing behaviour which can be described as 'nervous', 'anxious', tense, highly strung, and which is capable of psychological explanation.

NORMS Standards of performance relating to a group of scores in a test, or tests.

PEER GROUP This refers to a group of people of the same or similar age.

PHONOGRAM A unit symbol, or a phonetic writing system standing for a speech sound, or a sequence of speech sounds without reference to meaning.

PROJECTION Another form of 'defence mechanism' used in psycho-analysis whereby thoughts, feelings and attitudes present in oneself are attributed unconsciously to other people and which would arouse unpleasant feeling in ourselves if they were recognised.

PSYCHOMETRICS The study and practice of mental testing or of measurement applied to mental tests.

PSYCHOTICISM—NORMALITY A dimension of personality. Popularly a psychotic person is 'mad', 'insane', incapable of insight and is out of touch with reality.

RATIONALISATION A process of justifying an action or event after it has occurred. Another 'defence mechanism' against self-accusation and for concealing true motivation.

RESISTANCE A technical term in pyscho-analysis which describes the opposition encountered during a personal analysis to the process of making unconscious matters conscious.

RESTRICTED CODE A system of language habits—contrasted with an elaborated code—supposedly typical of certain working class families. The code is characterised by abbreviated grammatical structures and by a restricted vocabulary.

SERVO-MECHANISM A self-regulating system. The difference between the present and the required state is automatically fed back into the system which is activated until the difference disappears.

STANDARDISED TEST A specially constructed mental test of ability, attainment, special aptitudes or personality which enables statistically based norms of performance to be constructed. This enables individual scores to be compared with an average or mean.

TOUGH-MINDED—TENDER-MINDED Another dimension of personality—contrasting an unsentimental, practical, strong-willed, vigorous and not-easily-swayed person with one who is acutely sensitive, easily moved to sympathy and who is sentimental and compassionate.

# Appendix A

## Some Useful Books and Pamphlets for a Careers Adviser or Careers Teacher


*The Peacock Book of Careers for Girls*, Ruth Miller, Penguin 1966

*Careers for Boys*, Gavin Brown, Pan Books 1964

*Careers for Girls*, Gavin Brown, Pan Books 1964

Choice of Career booklets, HMSO (esp. No. 1 *Choosing your Career*)

*Careers—a memorandum on openings and training for girls and women*, Women Employment Federation, 251 Brompton Road, London, S.W.3

*Which University?* Cornmarket Press 1968

*National Union of Teachers Careers Guide*, 1969

*Prospect*, a magazine for careers advisers, Cornmarket Press (issued every three weeks)

*Opportunities after O Level*, Ed. by K. Newton and S. Abrams for the Advisory Centre for Education, 1965

*Careers Guidance in Schools*, HMSO 1965

*Directory of Further Education*, Cornmarket Press 1968

*Careers Guide*, Seventh Edition, HMSO 1968

*A Compendium of University Entrance Requirements*, The Association of Commonwealth Universities, 36 Gordon Square, London, W.C.1

*A Compendium of Advanced Courses in Technical Colleges*, published annually by the Regional Advisory Council for England and Wales, Tavistock House, Tavistock Square, London, W.C.1

*The Directory of Opportunities for Graduates*, Cornmarket Press 1966

*The Directory of Opportunities for School Leavers*, Cornmarket Press 1968

*Careers Encyelopaedia*, P.J. Edmonds (Ed.), Macmillan and Cleaver 1968

*The Youth Employment Service 1965-68*, HMSO 1968

*Young School Leavers*, *Schools Councils Enquiry*, HMSO 1968

*Teamwork in Careers Guidance*, R. D. Salter-Davies (Trends in Education) HMSO October 1966

*The Psychology of Study*, C. A. Mace, Penguin Second Ed. 1967

*How to Study*, H. Maddox, Pan Books Rev. Ed. 1967

*How to Study* (Obtainable from Sandbach School, Cruse Road, Sandbach, Cheshire price 5p)

*Inside Information on Career Opportunities*, J. Tomlinson and J. Moggridge, Dickens Press 1970 (25p)

# Appendix B

## Some Information about Counselling Developments in other Fields

It is useful for the School Counsellor to be aware of counselling developments in other related fields.

A student counselling and guidance service is beginning to be introduced into universities and some already have student counsellors appointed (e.g. Cambridge and Brunel Universities). G. W. Parkyn (*Success and Failure at the University*, Volume II, New Zealand Council for Educational Research, Wellington, New Zealand) advocates that such a system should be available to help students whose performance was disappointing, and it is likely that, as well as alleviating personal distress among students, the failure rate might be substantially reduced. *A Handbook on British Student Health Services* (Pitman Medical 1965) by N. Malleson gives information on student counselling services for this country. F. C. Palmer (*Student Guidance* Longmans 1965) describes some of the problems in developing a counselling service for students in a College of Further Education and pleads for an extension of this work in similar establishments; in particular lower down the educational ladder as he found many students who could have been helped much earlier in their schools (p.42).

*Counselling Services for Young People* (Standing Conference of National Voluntary Youth Organisation, 26 Bedford Square, London, W.C.1. 3rd revised edition, January 1968) is a useful survey of various attempts in this country to introduce counselling services for young people.

AMICI is a voluntary student-counsel service designed to offer pastoral counselling to people under the age of 25. For further information write to Kenneth Hodgson, MA, Townshend, 80 Hollies Avenue, West Byfleet, Surrey.

A report on a pilot project in Europe to test the value of special counselling services for the long term unemployed and frequent job-changers, is described by G. Williams *Counselling for Special Groups* (Organisation for Economic Co-operation and Development, Paris

1967). The outcome of this counselling was such that a favourable view is taken of its possible extension for similar problems.

*Marriage Guidance* by J. H. Wallis offers a sound guide to the principles and practice in any field of personal counselling.

# Appendix C

## Some Useful Addresses

*AMICI* A voluntary student-counsel service. K. W. Hodgson, Sec., Townshend, 80 Hollies Avenue, West Byfleet, Surrey

*Advisory Centre for Education* (ACE), 57 Russell Street, Cambridge

*Assessment and Research Centre*, Victory House, 99-101 Regent Street, London, W.1

*Association of Child Psychotherapists* (non-medical), Burgh House, New End Square, London, N.W.3

*Association of Educational Psychologists*, Hon. Sec. Mrs J. M. Currie, 3 Grange Court, Felling, Gateshead, County Durham

*Association of Psychotherapists*, 411 Upper Richmond Road, London, S.W.15

*British Film Institute*, 81 Dean Street, London, W.1

*BBC Further Education Liaison Officer*, PO Box 1AA, Broadcasting House, London, W.1

*British Psychological Society*, 18-19 Albemarle Street, London, W1X 4DN

*British Red Cross Society*, 14 and 15 Grosvenor Crescent, London, S.W.1

*British Student Health Association*, Hon. Sec. Dr S. E. Finlay, Leeds University Student Health Service, Leeds, 2

*Careers Research and Advisory Centre*, 25 Bateman Street, Cambridge

*Central Council for Health Education*, Tavistock House South, Tavistock Square, London, W.C.1

*Central Council of Physical Recreation*, 26 Park Crescent, London, W.1

*Comprehensive Schools Committee*, 209 Belsize Road, London N.W.6

*Confederation of Associations for the Advancement of State Education*, c/o G. Somerset, 42 Meadow Hill Road, Kings Norton, Birmingham 30

*Cornmarket Group Careers Centre*, Career Analysts, 27 Gloucester Place, London, W.1

*Council for Children's Welfare*, 23 Marlborough Place, London, N.W.8

*Council for Education in World Citizenship*, 25 Clarke Street, London, W.1

*Duke of Edinburgh's Award Scheme*, 2 Old Queen Street, London, S.W.1

*Home and School Council*, c/o G. Bond, Derwent College, University of York, Heslington, York

*International Round Table of Educational Counselling and Vocational Guidance*, Organising Sec., H. Z. Hoxter, Youth Employment Officer, 6 High Street South, East Ham, London, E.6

*Ministry of Labour Occupational Guidance Units*, Almack House, 26-28 King Street, London, S.W.1

*National Association of Careers Teachers*, c/o R. P. Heppell, South Shields Grammar/Technical School for Boys, South Shields, County Durham

*National Association of Educational Counsellors*, Hon. Sec., R. G. Lane, 34 Rothesay Avenue, Newcastle, Staffs

*National Association for Gifted Children*, 21 Montague Street, Portman Square, London, W.1

*National Association for Mental Health*, 39 Queen Anne Street, London, W.1

*National Association of Parent/Teacher Associations*, 75 Primrose Hill Court, King Henry's Road, London, N.W.3

*National Bureau for Co-operation in Child Care*, Adam House, 1 Fitzroy Square, London, W.1

*National Council of Social Service*, 26 Bedford Square, London, W.C.1

*National Council for the Unmarried Mother with her Child*, 255 Kentish Town Road, London, N.W.5

*National Foundation for Educational Research*, The Mere, Upton Park, Slough, Bucks

*National Institute of Industrial Psychology*, 14 Welbeck Street, London, W.1

*National Institute for Social Work Training*, Mary Ward House, 5-7 Tavistock Place, London, W.C.1

*National Marriage Guidance Council*, 58 Queen Anne Street, London, W.1

*National Society for Mentally Handicapped Children*, 84-86 Chancery Lane, London, W.C.2

*Outward Bound Trust*, 73 Great Peter Street, London, S.W.1

*Public Schools Appointments Bureau*, 17 Queen Street, London, W.1

*Royal Society of Health*, 90 Buckingham Palace Road, London, S.W.1

*Social Work Advisory Service*, 26 Bloomsbury Way, London, W.C.1

*Voluntary Service Overseas*, 18 Northumberland Avenue, London, W.C.2

In addition there are many local agencies who may help school counsellors and most teachers are aware of these various voluntary and statutory organisations (see list at end of Holden, 46).

# Appendix D

## There are four full-time one year university courses which train experienced teachers for school counselling posts. These are (in order of starting up):–

(i) *Keele University Institute of Education.* This was the first course of its kind started up by Mr C. J. Gill in October 1965, and offers a Diploma in the Advanced Study of Education with special reference to Counselling.

(ii) *Reading University Institute of Education.* This course was started in October 1966.

(iii) *Exeter University of Education.* This is a one year course offering a Diploma of Education (Educational Guidance and Counselling). This course started in October 1966.

(iv) *The University of Swansea Institute of Education.* This course started in October 1969, and offers a one year course for a Diploma in School Counselling.

Those interested in finding out further details are advised to write for current prospectuses.

There are other educational institutions offering a variety of courses with a counselling component. A list of these is available in Holden (p.208).

# Appendix E

## EXAMPLE OF A TESTING PROGRAMME

| *Age of Child* | | *Comments* |
|---|---|---|
| 8 | A measure of reading ability. A measure of verbal intelligence, e.g. NFER Primary Verbal[1]. | Best given individually either Vernon, Schonell and Neale. Reading disability problems can be identified and remedial reading programmes started. |
| 9 | A group measure of reading ability is probably sufficient for most children (e.g. NFER Sentence Reading Test 1) supplemented by an individual reading test where necessary.<br>A group measure of verbal intelligence e.g. NFER Primary Verbal 1.<br>A measure of arithmetical/mathematical ability, e.g. NFER Arithmetic Progress Test A2. | |
| 10 | A measure of intelligence, e.g. NFER Primary Verbal 2.<br>A measure of English Ability, e.g. English Progress Test B2 (NFER).<br>A measure of mathematical ability, e.g. NFER Junior Mathematical Test C3. | |
| 11 | Either a battery of closed tests or a measure of intelligence, e.g. NFER Primary Verbal 3. | Closed tests are supplied for the purposes of secondary school selection and are not available for general use. |
| | A measure of English, e.g. NFER.<br>A measure of mathematical ability, e.g. NFER Intermediate Diagnostic Arithmetic Test 1. | This test can be used either with or without a time limit and can be used to diagnose mathematical strengths and weaknesses. |

| *Age of Child* | | *Comments* |
|---|---|---|
| 13 | A battery of objective tests (giving measures of various aspects of mental ability such as number ability, verbal ability), e.g. JRM Differential Test Battery (DTB).<br>A measure of reading skill is probably best given by an individual test such as the Vernon, which has a high ceiling and can give a measure of reading skill to a reading age of 19 years. | Any test battery here needs special training (e.g. such a training is available at the Independent Assessment and Research Centre, 5 Tavistock Place, London, W.C.1. Further information about courses here can be obtained from the Director).<br>Vernon Graded Vocabulary Word Reading Test (106), University of London Press. |

An alternative would be to have a measure of general ability (e.g. NFER Secondary Verbal 1), a measure of English ability (e.g. NFER English Progress F) and a measure of mathematical ability (e.g. NFER Mathematics Test 1). As an alternative to the individual reading test suggested above, a group reading test (such as the NFER Secondary Reading Tests 1-3 may be given).

Any further objective testing after the age of fourteen can be arranged either by repeating the battery of tests used previously (e.g. the Morrisby Tests) or by arranging a special testing programme in consultation with the school psychologist.

As an alternative to this suggested scheme for use in the Primary School, N. France and S. Wiseman have devised a battery of short, untimed tests which are easy to use, are compact in one test booklet and which offer measures of different abilities. The 32-page booklet contains a variety of tests for children to do in the seven to ten year age group and which they can complete at their own pace over a period of two weeks. For further details see N. France and S. Wiseman, 'An Educational Guidance Programme for the Primary School', *B. J. Ed. Psych.* June 1966. Vol. 36. Pt. 2, 210-226.

# Bibliography

## Books, Pamphlets and Articles

1. Andry, R. G. *Delinquency and Parental Pathology* (Methuen 1960)

2. Allport-Vernon-Lindzey *Study of Values* (3rd ed. Houghton-Mifflin 1960)

3. Argyle, M. *The Psychology of Inter-Personal Behaviour* (Penguin 1967)

4. Bantock, G. H. *Education in an Industrial Society* (Faber 1963)

5. Bantock, G. H. *Culture, Industrialisation and Education* (Routledge 1968)

6. Bartlett, F. C. *The Study of Society* (Routledge 1939)

7. Bernstein, B. *Social Structure, Language and Learning* Educ. Res. 3 (3) (1961)

8. Bernstein, B. 'Aspects of Language and Learning in the Genesis of the Social Process' *J. Child Psychol. Psychiat.* 1 (4), 313–324 (1961)

9. Borger, H. & Seaborne A. E. M. *The Psychology of Learning* (Penguin 1966)

10. Bott, E. *Family and Social Network* (Tavistock 1964)

11. Bowlby, J. *Child Care and the Growth of Love* (Penguin 1953)

12. Boy, A. V. and Pine, G. J. *Client-Centred Counselling in the Secondary School* (Houghton Mifflin 1963)

13. British Psychological Society. Various pamphlets as follows: *The School Psychological Service; Principles Governing the Employment of Psychological Tests* and *Clinical Instruments; Psychological Tests; Technical Recommendations for Psychological and Educational Tests.*

14. Broadbent, D. E. *Behaviour* (Eyre & Spottiswoode 1961)

15. Brown, J. A. C. *Freud and the Post-Freudians* (Penguin 1961)

16. Butcher, H. J. *Human Intelligence* (Methuen 1968)

17. Carter, M. *Into Work* (Penguin 1966)

18. Cartwright, D. 'Achieving Change in People' *Hum. Relat.* 4. (4), 388–391 (1951)

19. Caspari, I. E. 'Counselling—definitions and dilemmas' *The New Era*, 49 (9) (1968)

20. Chanter, A. G. *Sex Education in the Primary School* (Macmillan 1966)

21. Cooper, M. G. 'School Refusal' *Educ. Res.* 8 (2), 115–127 (1966)

22. 'Counselling in the Schools' *Working Paper No. 15. School Council* (HMSO 1967)

23. Craft, M., Raynor J. & Cohen L. *Linking Home and School* (Longmans 1967)

24. Davis, D. R. *Introduction to Psychopathology* (Oxford Medical Publications 1952)

25. Daws, P. 'What will the School Counsellor do?' *Educ. Res.* 9, (2) (1967)

26. Daws, P. *A Good Start in Life* (Careers Research and Advisory Centre 1968)

27. Douglas, J. W. B. *The Home and the School* (MacGibbon & Kee 1964)

28. Douglas, J. W. B., Ross, J. M. & Simpson, H. R. *All our Future* (Peter Davies 1968)

29. Elvin, H. L. *Education & Contemporary Society* (Watts 1965)

30. Evans, K. M. *Sociometry and Education* (Routledge 1962)

31. Evans, K. M. 'Sociometry in School, I Sociometric Techniques' *Educ. Res.* 6, (1) (1963)

32. Evans, K. M. 'Sociometry in School, II Application' *Educ. Res.* 6, (2) (1964)

33. Evans, K. M. *Planning Small-Scale Research* (NFER 1968)

34. Eysenck, H. J. *Uses and Abuses of Psychology* (Penguin 1953)

35. Eysenck, H. J. *Behaviour Therapy & the Neuroses* (Pergamon 1960)

36. Eysenck, H. J. *Know your Own I.Q.* (Penguin 1962)

37. Eysenck, H. J. *Fact & Fiction in Psychology* (Penguin 1965)

38. Fleming, C. M. *Adolescence* (second ed. Routledge 1963)

39. Forder, A. (Ed.) *Hall's Social Services of England and Wales* (Routledge 1969)

40. Freeman, R. St. J. & Freeman, H. A. *Counselling, A Bibliography* (Scarecrow Press 1964)

41. Gill, C. J. 'The Trained School Counsellor' *The New Era* 48 (9) (November 1967)

42. Government Reports:
Underwood *Maladjusted Children* (HMSO 1955)
Robbins *Reports on Higher Education* (HMSO 1963)
Newsom *Half our Future* (HMSO 1963)
Gittens *Primary Education in Wales* (HMSO 1967)
Plowden *Children and their Primary Schools* (HMSO 1967)
Summerfield *Psychologists in Educaion Services* (HMSO 1968)
Seebohm *Local Authority . . . Personal Social Services* (HMSO 1968)

43. Gross, R. (Ed.) *British Secondary Education* (Oxford University Press 1965)

44. Hall, R. K. & Lauwerys, J. A. (Eds.) *Yearbook of Education* (Evans 1955)

45. Halmos, P. *Towards a Measure of Man* (Routledge 1957)

46. Halmos, P. (Ed.) 'Papers on the Teaching of Personality Development' *Sociological Review Monograph No. 2* (University College of N. Staffs 1959)

47. Halmos, P. *The Faith of the Counsellors* (Constable 1965)

48. Holden, A. *Teachers as Counsellors* (Constable 1969)

49. Hudson, L. *Contrary Imaginations* (Methuen 1966)

50. Hughes, P. M. 'Guidance and Counselling in British Education' *The European Teacher* (July 1968)

51. Ingleby, A. H. 'Counselling Students' *Marriage Guidance* (March 1968)

52. Jahoda, M. *Current Concepts of Positive Mental Health* (Basic Books 1958)

53. Jones, A. 'An experiment in Counselling in a London Setting' *The New Era* 48 (9) (November 1968)

54. Jones, H. *Crime in a Changing Society* (Penguin 1965)

55. Keir, G. 'A History of Child Guidance' *Br. J. Educ. Psychol.* XXII, (1) (1952)

56. Keir, G. *Adventures in Reading* Teacher's Handbook (Oxford University Press 1952)

57. Kellmer Pringle, M. L. 'An experiment in Parent-Staff Discussions' *Educ. Rev.* IX, 128–135 (1957)

58. Khan, J. H. *Human Growth and the Development of Personality* (Pergamon 1967)

59. Khan, J. H. *The Child Guidance Clinic* (NAMH, 39 Queen Anne Street, London, W.1)

60. Lawton, D. *Social Class, Language and Education* (Routledge 1968)

61. Lees, A. 'Looking towards Integration. Experiments by a Child Guidance Centre' *Br. J. Psychiat. Soc. Wk.* IX, (3) (1968)

62. Leissner, A. *Family Advice Services* (Longman 1967)

63. Lovell, K. *Educational Psychology and Children* (Tenth ed. 1968 University of London Press)

64. Lovell, K. *An introduction to Human Development* (Macmillan 1968)

65. Lytton, H. *School Counselling & Counsellor Education in the United States* (NFER 1968)

66. Lytton, H. & Craft, M. *Guidance and Counselling in British Schools* (Edward Arnold 1969)

67. MacLean, I. *Child Guidance and the School* (Methuen 1966)

68. O'Connor, K. *Learning: an Introduction* (Macmillan 1968)

69. Oldfield, R. C. *The Psychology of the Interview* (Third ed. Methuen 1947)

70. 'Parent/Teacher Relations in Primary Schools' *Educational Survey No. 5* (HMSO 1968)

71. Pedley, F. H. (Ed.) *Education and Social Work* (Pergamon 1968)

72. Pidgeon, D. 'The Design, Construction and Use of Standardised Tests' *Educ. Res.* 111, (2) (1961)

73. Pidgeon, D. & Yates, A. *An Introduction to Educational Measurement* (Routledge 1968)

74. Rachman, S. 'Introduction to Behaviour Therapy' *Behav. Res. Ther.* 1, (1), 3–16 (1963)

75. Richardson, E. *Group Study for Teachers* (Routledge 1967)

76. Roberts, F. H. 'An Experiment in Counselling' *The New Era* 49 (9) (November 1968)

77. Roberts, G. 'The Teaching of Personal Relationships in Wiltshire Secondary Schools' *The New Era* 48 (9) (November 1967)

78. Rodger, A. 'Planning for Vocational Guidance' *Occup. Psychol.* 13 (1939)

79. Roe, M. C. *Survey into the Progress of Maladjusted Pupils* (Inner London Education Authority 1965)

80. Rogers, C. R. *Counselling & Psychotherapy* (Houghton Mifflin 1942)

81. Rogers, C. R. *Client-Centred Therapy* (Houghton Mifflin 1951)

82. Rogers, C. R. 'A Theory of Therapy Personality and Interpersonal Relationships' in Koch. S. (Ed.) *Psychology: A Study of Science* Vol. III, 184–256 (McGraw Hill 1959)

83. Rowe, A. W. 'Counselling in a Comprehensive School' *New Education* 4 (2) (February 1968)

84. Schofield, M. *Sexual Behaviour of Young People* (Longmans 1965)

85. Semeonoff, B. 'Projective Techniques in Selection for Counselling' *Hum. Relat.* 2, 113–122 (1958)

86. Sharp, J. 'Care of the Individual at Egremont' *The New Era* 48 (9) (1967)

87. Shields, R. 'Guidance & Counselling' *The New Era* 49 (1) (January 1968)

88. Shouksmith, G. & Taylor, J. W. 'The Effect of Counselling on the Achievement of High Ability Pupils' *Br. J. Educ. Psychol.* 34 (1) (1964)

89. Sidney, E. & Brown, M. *The Skills of Interviewing* (Tavistock 1966)

90. Skinner, B. F. *Science & Human Behaviour* (Macmillan 1953)

91. Skinner, B. F. *Cumulative Record* (Methuen 1959)

92. Slavson, S. R. *Child-Centred Group Guidance of Parents* (International University Press 1960)

93. Southgate, V. 'Approaching i.t.a. results with caution' *Educ. Res.* VII, (2) (1965)

94. Stern, H. H. 'Parent Education' *University of Hull Studies in Education* & UNESCO Institute of Education (1960)

95. Stewart, L. H. & Warnath, C. F. *The Counsellor and Society* (Houghton Mifflin 1965)

96. Storr, A. *The Integrity of the Personality* (Penguin 1963)

97. Stott, D. H. *Delinquency & Human Nature* (Carnegie United Kingdom Trust 1950)

98. Stott, D. H. *Saving Children from Delinquency* (University of London Press 1952)

99. Stott, D. H. *Studies of Troublesome Children* (Tavistock 1966)

100. Stuart, F. A. 'Counselling in Personal Relationships in Secondary Schools' *The New Era* 48 (9) (November 1967)

101. Taconis, L. 'The Role of the Contemporary Father in rearing Young Children' *Educ. Res.* 11, (2) (1969)

102. Tame, H. W. *Peter & Pamela Grow Up* (Darwen Findlayson 1960)

103. Tanner, J. M. *Growth & Adolescence* (Blackwell Scientific Publications, Oxford 1955)

104. Tanner, J. M. *Education & Physical Growth* (University of London Press 1961)

105. Taylor, H. J. F. 'Issues in School Counselling' *The New Era* 49 (6) (June 1968)

106. Taylor, H. J. F. 'The School Counsellor as a Personal Counsellor?' *The New Era* 49, (10) (December 1968)

107. Taylor, W. *The Secondary Modern School* (Faber 1963)

108. Tizard, J. 'Questionnaire Methods of Maladjustment' *Br. J. Educ. Psychol.* 38, (1) (1968)

109. Tyerman, M. J. *Truancy* (University of London Press 1968)

110. Vaizey, J. *Education in the Modern World* (Weidenfield and Nicholson 1967)

111. Veness, T. *School Leavers* (Methuen 1962)

112. Vernon, P. E. *The Standardisation of a Graded Word Reading Test* (University of London Press 1938)

113. Vernon, P. E. *Personality Tests and Assessments* (Methuen 1953)

114. Vernon, P. E. *Intelligence and Attainment Tests* (University of London Press 1960)

115. Vernon, P. E. *The Structure of Human Abilities* (Second Ed. Methuen 1961)

116. Vernon, P. E. 'What is Potential Ability?' *Bull. Br. Psychol. Soc.* 21 (73) (1968)

117. Wagner, M. K. 'A case of public masturbation treated by operant conditioning' *J. Child Psychol. Psychiat.* 9, 61/65 (1968)

118. Wall, W. D. *Education & Mental Health* (Harrap for UNESCO 1955)

119. Wall, W. D. *Adolescents in School & Society* (NFER 1968)

120. Wall, W. D. *Psychological Services for Schools* (Hanburg Institute of Education for UNESCO 1956)

121. Wallis, J. H. 'Marriage Counselling and the Professions' *Marriage Guidance* 10, (6) (November 1966); 10 (7) (January 1967); 10 (8) (March 1967)

122. Wallis, J. H. *Marriage Guidance* (Routledge 1968)

123. Warburton, F. W. 'The Measurement of Personality' *Educ. Res.* IV (2) (1962)

124. Wechsler, D. *Wechsler Intelligence Scale for Children* (Psychological Corporation 1949)

125. Wechsler, D. *The Measurement of Adult Intelligence* (Williams & Wilkins, Fourth Ed. 1958)

126. Wiegersma, S. & Barr, F. 'Interest Testing in Educational and Vocational Guidance' *Educ. Res.* 2 (1), 39/64 (1959)

127. Willmott, P. *Consumers Guide to the Social Services* (Pelican 1967)

128. Wilson, B. R. 'The Teacher's Role—a Sociological Analysis' *Br. J. Sociol.* 13, 15/32 (1962)

129. Wilson, J. *Education and the Concept of Mental Health* (Routledge 1968)

130. Winnicott, D. W. 'Adolescence' *The New Era* 43, 145/151 (1962)

131. Wiseman, S. *Education and Environment* (Manchester University Press 1964)

132. Woody, R. H. 'British Behavioural Counselling' *Educ. Res.* 10 (3) (1968)

133. Woody, R. H. 'Integrating Behaviour Therapy and Psychotherapy' *Br. J. Med. Psychol.* 41 (3), 261/266

134. Wrenn, C. G. *The Counsellor in a Changing World* (American Personnel and Guidance Association 1962)

135. Young, M. & Willmot, P. *Family and Kinship in East London* (Penguin 1957)

136. Zahran, H. A. S. 'The Self Concept in the Psychological Guidance of Adolescents' *Br. J. Educ. Psychol.* 37 (2) (1967)

137. Zangwill, O. *Introduction to Modern Psychology* (Second Ed. Methuen 1962)

# Index

adolescence, 69-71
Allport-Vernon-Lindzey, Study of Values, 90, 153
Anastasi, A., 95
Anderson, J. and Kerr, A.H., 97
Andry, R.G., 133, 153
Argyle, M., 17, 153

Bailey, S.K., 140
Balbernie, R., 140
Bantock, G.H., 31, 153
Bartlett, F.C., 153
Beck, J.C., 73
behaviourism, 62
Bernstein, B., 86, 153
Blos, P., 73
Borger, H. and Seaborne, A.E.M., 73, 153
Bott, E., 120, 121, 140, 153
Bowlby, J., 56, 133, 141, 153
Boy, A.V. and Pine, G.J., 26, 32, 119, 153
British Psychological Society, 153
Broadbent, D.E., 56, 64, 73, 153
Brown, J.A.C., 73, 153
Buros, 95
Butcher, H.J., 153

Careers Guidance Service, 24, 40ff., 52
Careers Research and Advisory Centre (CRAC), 32
Carter, M., 32, 47, 53, 123, 125, 127, 140, 153
Cartwright, D., 114, 153
case conference, 37
Caspari, I.E., 34, 36, 153
Chanter, H.G., 68, 73, 153
Chazan, M., 139
Child Care Officer, 45, 50
Child Guidance, 48, 49, 51, 54, 132, 135
Children and Young Persons' Act, 51, 53, 139
communication breakdown, 38
comprehensive schools, 13
conditioning, 62
Cooper, M.G., 137, 141, 154
counselling, 15, 16, 17, 20, 23, 138
 definition of, 21, 103
 effectiveness of, 4, 28
 group, 112ff.
 and parents, 128ff.
 roles in, 22
 and teaching, 16ff.
Craft, M., Raynor, J., and Cohen, L., 31, 140, 154
Cronbach, L.J., 95

Davis, D.R., 108, 109, 154
Davis, D.R. and Asher Cashdon, 96
Dawes, P., 22, 24, 43, 44, 47, 53, 154
Dawkins, J., 73
Douglas, J.W.B., 11, 14, 154
Downing, J., 96

Edgehill College of Education, 48
Education Welfare Officer, 45, 49, 136
Educational Psychologist, 45, 51
Elvin, H.L., 13, 31, 154
Evans, K.M., 96, 97, 119, 154
Eysenck, H.J., 62, 65, 73, 82, 99, 154

family, 14, 120ff., 133, 134
Fleming, C.M., 11, 154
Flugel, J.C., 140
Forder, A., 53, 154
Freeman, H.A., 32, 154
Freeman, R.S.J., 32, 154
Freud, S., 56

Gathercole, C.E., 95
Gill, C.J., 16, 154
Gittens Report, 154
government reports, 154
Gross, R., 12, 155
group counselling, 115, 116
guidance, 18ff.
Guidance Unit, Reading University, 48
Gulliford, R., 96

Hall, R.K. and Lauwerys, J.A., 32, 155
Halmos, P., 60, 73, 155
Hoard, M.L., 118
Holbrook, D., 118
Holden, A., 32, 119, 128, 155
Hudson, L., 56, 96, 155
Hughes, P.M., 32, 155
Hughes, T., 31

Independent Assessment and Research Centre, 95
Ingleby, A.H., 109, 110, 155
intelligence, 82
interests, 89
interviewing, 98
Irvine, E., 52

Jahoda, M., 27, 155
Jones, A., 24, 33, 155
Jones, H., 127, 155

Kaye, B., and Rogers, I., 119
Keir, G., 19, 96, 155
Kellmer Pringle, M., 32, 129, 141, 155
Khan, J., 54, 141, 155
Klein, M., 56

Lauwerys, A., 32, 155
Lawton, D., 87, 96, 155
Lees, A., 31, 49, 111, 155
Leissner, A., 53, 155
Lovell, K., 72, 73, 96, 155
Lytton, H., 53, 155

Maclean, I., 54, 155
maladjustment, 25, 27, 132, 135
Malleson, N., 140, 146
mental health, 27
Morris, J.M., 96
Morrisby Differential Test Battery, 95

National Association of Educational Counsellors, 21, 26
National Institute of Industrial Psychology, 41
National Marriage Guidance Council, 20, 26, 32
Newsom Report, 20, 154
N.I.I.P. 7-Point Plan, 42, 43, 47

O'Connor, K., 73, 156
Oldfield, R.C., 98, 119, 156

Parents and Counselling, 128
Parkin, G.W., 145
Pedley, F.H., 47, 53, 87, 139, 156
personality difficulties, 11
personality tests, 90
Pidgeon, D., 78, 79, 96, 156
Plowden Report, 154
Probation Officer, 45, 50
Psychiatric Social Worker, 45, 49, 51
psycho-analysis, 59
psychotherapist, 51, 108
psychotherapy, 115

Rachman, S., 62, 73, 156
Ravenette, A.T., 96
Rawlings, G., 32
Rayner, J.M., 53, 154
Reading, 83
reinforcement, 63
Richardson, E., 119, 156
Robbins Report, 86, 154
Roberts, F.H., 18, 24, 104, 105, 107, 156
Roberts, G., 23, 156
Rodger, A., 41, 42, 44, 53, 100, 156
Roe, M.C., 135, 156
Rogers, C.R., 57, 73, 107, 115, 119, 156
Rothwell-Miller Interest Blank, 90, 95
Rowe, A.W., 24, 53, 156
Rutter, M., 90, 96
Ryecroft, C., 72

Schofield, M., 156
School Counsellor, 16, 21, 26, 34, 35, 45, 135
school psychological service, 51, 54
Schools Council, 154
Seaborne, E.A.M., 153
Seebohm Report, 48, 53, 154
self-concepts, 115
Semeonoff, B., 106, 156
sex education, 37, 67ff., 72
Sharp, J., 24, 156
Shields, J.B., 32
Shields, R., 18, 156
Shouksmith, G. and Taylor, J.W., 29, 86, 156
Skinner, B.F., 63, 73, 156
Slavson, S.R., 130, 141, 157
Social Services Act 1970, 48, 50, 53, 126
social worker, 47
sociometry, 91–93
Southgate, V., 72, 96, 157
S.R.A. programmed reading material, 80, 95
Stern, H.H., 128, 129, 141, 157
Stewart, L.H. and Warnath, C.F., 32, 38, 39, 53, 119
Storr, A., 73, 157
Stott, D.H., 25, 90, 96, 133, 134, 141, 157
Stuart, F.A., 26, 157
Summerfield Report, 26, 140, 154
Sydney, E. and Brown, M., 100, 102, 119, 156

Taconis, L., 133, 141, 157
Tame, H.W., 73, 157
Tanner, J.M., 66, 73, 157
Taylor, H.J.F., 22, 157
Taylor, J.W., 29, 156
Taylor, W., 18, 157
Teaching, 17, 18
test programme, 88, 89, 151
tests, 74, 78
Tizard, J., 90, 157
traits, 64
Trotter, W., 118
truancy and school refusal, 136
Tyerman, M.J., 136, 141, 157

Underwood Report, 25, 26, 132, 154

Vaizey, J., 31, 157
Venables, Ethel, 33
Veness, T., 44, 53, 157
Vernon, P.E., 65, 82, 85, 95, 96, 157

Wagner, M.K., 63, 73, 158
Wall, W.D., 20, 54, 70, 73, 97, 158
Wallis, J.H., 26, 32, 119, 158
Warburton, F.W., 91, 96, 158
Watts, A.G., 32
Wechsler, D., 158
Wiegersman, S. and Barr, F., 96, 158
Williams, K.A., 119
Willmott, P., 53, 158
Wilson, B.R., 17, 158
Wilson, J., 27, 158
Wimble, A.W., 48
Winnicott, D.W., 71, 158
Wiseman, S., 88, 158
Woody, R.H., 62, 73, 158
Wrenn, C.G., 13, 31, 32, 158

Young, M., and Willmott, P., 14, 123, 158
Younghusband, E., 140
Youth Employment Service, 41, 46, 47, 52

Zahrahn, H.A.S., 115, 158
Zangwill, O., 55, 158